BOOK OF WILL AND WORLD
Foundation of Moral
Universalism

Anup Rej

BOOK OF WILL AND WORLD

Foundation of Moral Universalism

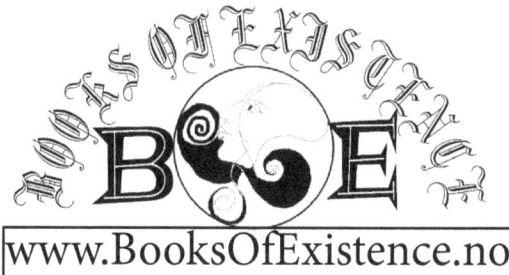

www.BooksOfExistence.no

Content

INTRODUCTION

Since the dawn of civilization the cosmic objects and the knowledge about the creation have decided the way man has chosen its social, cultural and political behavior and submitted itself to an authority outside the mortal sphere. The sun and the moon and the stars have played central roles in evoking their imagination about Heaven and the realm of the gods and goddesses. Their motions were believed to cause the earthly changes and influence the happenings on life. The cosmic forces were believed to bring destiny of life and death on the mortal sphere. The planets and their starry conjunctions also were studied carefully to presage the passages of events to come in the future. Those mortals, who delved in these affairs of the cosmos and its impact on the life on Earth, became the holy men, having power to foresee events beyond the present and suggest ways to appease the heavenly powers in order to circumvent the upcoming events and instead bring forth a more desirable result. Thus some mortals were assumed to possess the abilities to connect to the cosmic know-how and bring beneficent destiny to the earthlings. They became the priests and the mediators between Earth and Heaven. Their increased power over the mortals, fearful of the heavenly retributions, gave these holy men the liberty to expand on the knowledge of Heaven and the way things may have been ordained in order to fulfill the will of Heaven. The power of Heaven thus descended on these holy men, who executed their power in the society in the name of the heavenly creatures and orbs.

1

To make life more bearable and manageable for the earthlings against the natural forces challenging the conditions of survival of the mortal creatures, besides appeasing the gods with offerings and prayers, the society needed heroes who could fight against the calamities and the odds of life and make life more secure for survival. So came the semi-god like heroes who could bring comforts and security to the people by fighting floods, draughts, pestilence etc. and defending the society against invasions from outside intruders and ferocious beasts. They were assumed to possess some sort of divine power in their physical earthly incarnation. The societies were organized in collaboration with these holy persons and the divine-power carrying strong men. With the consolidation of power,supported by loyalty by the social members, some of them assumed authorities of controlling the resources in the society and with opportunities instituted laws and decrees with which they could perpetuate the control over wealth, political power, labour resources etc. Beliefs and thoughts were implanted in the society that could make the survival potential of the institutions controlling the society stronger. They became the bearer of the tradition and culture expressed through modes of worships, celebrations and festivals. This development of religion and politics gave birth to the priests, kings in the written history. The economic resources including landed proper-ties and religious wealths became concentrated in a very few hands, while the laymen were exploited and their labour were harnessed to serve the luxury and prosperity of the noble class. The holy men who collaborated with the kings and mighty men got their earthly rewards in terms of boosted recognition of their holiness and sanctity and sup-port of their other worldly activities. This continued till the days of feudalism.

As the knowledge of the world increased, and human beings developed seafaring technology and skill to navigate to distant lands, the com-munity of merchants, in search of wealth and fortune, rose who came to challenge this old power model of the feudal era. Unprecedented source of wealth found in other continents made them greedy for pow-er and they colluded with people of common interests to weaken the power of the noble men. They went to colonize far away lands in other continents and soon discovered that the world was not flat as they had

2

believed and the human beings did not live at the centre of the universe encircled by spheres controlled by the Divine forces. The power of gun, treachery, bribes, and conspiracy proved more powerful than any Divine blessings and faith in winning material power and secure one`s lot. The new scientific discoveries that the planetary spheres including the spheres of the sun and the moon were not moving around Earth, and may be no Divine power was causing the universe to move around, brought a new awakening of the earthlings about the nature of their existence and their place in the cosmos. With the increasing scientific knowledge, the beauty, harmony, and the music of the spheres became more and more doubtful and turned the knowledge- seeking human beings against the religious dogmatism and the hold of power of the religious clergies on the social and political affairs. They took the affairs of the world in their own hands instead. They robbed, looted, traded and made use of all unscrupulous means to gain wealth and found ways to make more wealth by lending the money at their disposal at high interests. Thus a modern banking system came in life. The idea was to make money out of "nothing" i.e. without working - just speculating and exploiting the needs of the monetary transactions in the exchange of commodities and paying for labors, which was in rising need in a commercially expanding world. Those who tried to hold on to the feudal values and ideas succumbed to the greed of the banking and the commercial class.

Then came the industrialization and the mechanization of the manufacturing industries, which brought more efficiency and competitiveness in gaining control of the market, which had already expanded globally with the rise of colonialism. More scientific knowledge poured in, more one discovered the irrelevance of any heavenly power and those holy men communicating with heaven in resolving the needs of the mortal life. Instead, the greed and the will to compete and be the winner of one`s own life by one`s own strength and deed became the moral epithet of those who wished to succeed. By that time science had also brought the knowledge about the creation of human beings through an evolutionary process starting from a primitive life form. The competitions in a free world was the essence of this evolutionary success. Those, who failed in the competition, where intelligence played a central role, had no guarantee for survival. It was intelligence, innovation, strategy and tactics to defeat the competitor which paved the way for survival and success. All those required qualities for success lay in no other heaven than in the human brain.

The scientific revolution, innovation in organizing banking and marketing sectors brought the end of the traditional feudal dominance. The bankers, and industrialists rose to throw the noble and holy men from the seats of power. The world was renewed through bloody revolutions and the power changed hands to the new men of the industrial age. The development of steam engines, ships, railways and automobiles accelerated the speed of economic revolution totally controlled by the imagination and dexterity of the scientific and innovative human beings. It brought a total change of the way the human beings had got accustomed to living in the previous centuries.

The fierce competition for winning territories which would supply industrial raw materials and cheap labor, and unhindered access to expanded markets for the produced goods, put the countries enjoying the bonanza of the industrial revolution at each others`s throe. The economic competitions and chaos resulted in the rise of Fascism, Nazism and Communism and it produced two World Wars in the first half of the twentieth century causing 60 -70 million deaths.

After the Nazis and Fascists were defeated in the Second World War, the coalition between the Capitalists and the Communists came to an end. Instead, the world got divided into two blocks: On one side there were the capitalists who believed in the power of accumulating capital by using the profits made by investing some capital and thus run the power house of the market capitalism; on the other side there were the communists who believed in the ownership of the means of production by the workers and freedom from the capitalist mode of exploitation where workers were deprived of ownership of goods that were based on their labor and toil.

The rivalries between these two blocks increased, which sped up the technological race: Bombers, rockets, missiles were followed by nuclear warheads. Bigger and bigger nuclear warheads were piled up on each side with the aim of delivering them with ICBMs from one continent to the other to bring a total annihilation of the one who would be hit. It was argued that it was the best strategy for peace in the world because knowing what may come from the other as retaliation for an attack would deter any aggression by any other country. This cold war lasted till the last decade of the twentieth century, when USSR broke up and the countries in the Eastern Europe became free from the Socialist Block. By then the communist China had also adopted market liberalization in the spirit of compromising with the capitalist ideology of free market economy.

Since this debacle of socialism and communism the world has been lifted in a new technological era with radio and television bringing news, entertainment, and advertisement of services and products to nearly all homes in all corners of the world. In these days democratic politics have become the business of media magnets in many parts of the world, where the idea of democracy has taken roots after the colonial powers have withdrawn. The greatest impact of the ideas of democracy has been the liberalization of the consumer market without state control, and allowing the people to tune on to their preferred media channels and choose the consumer culture that may best express their free will. Democracy has become a free market item, which is offered at sale prices in many Department stores. By roaming in these stores one may feel free and be willing to happily use the right to vote for the creators of such material showcases! No god can compete with the earthlings`offer of such consumer Paradise!

This opening up of the global consumer market is funneling investments into nations from other countries across the globe, without caring about any ideology or moral philosophy. In the spirit of evolutionary theory "the survival of the fittest"is the only criteria one needs to focus on in order to find one`s way through this market labyrinth. More gimmick, packaging, entertainment and show, of course, increase the potential for success. Now the whole world has joined this choir of the vibrant market culture, unlike the colonial days, when only a small part of the world had access to luxury items. Human will seems to be liberated from the hands of heaven and placed in the hands of the investors and technocrats who see the market as a roulette of accidents and chance - a game of Devil more than anything else.

It resonates well with modern creation theory of the universe. There is a consensus among the majority of the scientists today that the universe was created out of a big explosion called the "Big-Bang". There was no reason. It was just an accident that it occurred. It was equally an accident that the fundamental constants in nature were just right for the creation of the material world. Otherwise creation was not possible through the mediation of the natural laws. It was simply an accident that we exist.

Amidst these plethora of accidents from big-bang to our coming into existence as human beings, freedom is an accident, so is our will and so is our will immersed in the free-market paradise ...!

The trees of this paradise have spread branches even in our personal inner life. The market has entered through internet networking in the brain activities of the new generation. While surfing on the web, interacting in social networking pages, watching youtube videos and seeking information about anything in the world by using the modern technology, the invisible virtual market-demon has found its pathways to enter the brain from all sides whether one desires it or not. Like an incurable disease it has invaded the modern mind and taking toll on the cultural behaviors of the human beings. Advertisements of consumer products, including the choices of the partners for life, have spread their networks controlled by the market forces, from which the private moments of people are not spared.

The nature of competitions have taken a different character now. The once underdeveloped countries, ruled by the colonial powers before the World Wars, have taken the front seats in the "automobiles" driving the economic developments of the globe. The large number of consumers in these populous nations are determining the flows of the financial capital investments away from the western countries to these markets. The economic power balance is tilting in favour of these nations and replacing the culture and traditions all over the world by a hunger for copying the western lifestyle. The western powers have become apprehensive that they may loose power to the people whom they had ruled by using their technological edges brought by the industrial civilization. The prospect of a new economic world-order has appeared in the horizon, which may threaten the supremacy of the power of the West - especially the United States, who has militarily and economically ruled the world after the Second World War. Instead of the capitalist and socialist blocks confronting each other, now the competition has turned into a struggle for economic supremacy between the West and the developing nations experiencing accelerated pace of economic growth. At this moment, when world is facing the prospect of a geopolitical transition of power from the hands of the West to the populous nations of the world in Asia, the control of the energy resources and innovation of new energy sources are becoming more and more precarious. The effect of this tension is becoming visible in the political turmoils in the Middle East, which is clad in the name of opening up democratic rules and waged by exploiting the rivalries among religious factions and the secular elements in the population. The military technological superiority of the West still tries to decide the outcome in conflicts in order to keep the power to dominate the globe in the hands of the Western powers.

The increased globalization of the economy and integration of the free-market across nations of the world have generated needs for more energy-especially burning of coal and oil resulting in undesirable consequence of its impacts on the climate on Earth. The prospect of mass migration due to climate generated events and its repercussions in the social-political stabilities of vulnerable countries have become matters of global concern these days. The needs for economic growth and production for the consumer market to maintain the political stability and, in the end, come out victorious in the geopolitical struggle are becoming the decisive factors to take into account into national policy makings of countries caught in rivalry for power.

In a world today, when no one should doubt any more that the destiny of life on Earth rests in the hands of human beings, who possess the power of technology and scientific innovations, rather than any power of Heaven and benevolence of God, why should man seek for guidance outside the sphere of the market practices which bears the signs of modern life? When free competitions without moral constraints have become the factors generating economic growths, and human relations are receiving attentions like products, which need to be promoted, advertised, consumed or cast off in order to integrate oneself in the global cultural arena, where could be the way to conceive oneself as anything else but an animal specie still caught into a blind evolutionary struggle driven by accidents and chances?

Anyway, who are our enemies, against whom we should fight in order to guard our sanctums of existence? Besides the natural forces, are there any other enemies who may be threatening our home? Is there any immediate calamity we need to give our attentions to? What is the direction in which we should move from where we find ourselves? Is there anywhere to go, or are we caught up in an accidental whirlwind of time, that may take us to paths not chosen by our limited understanding of ourselves? Mind cries to know the answers: Where are we really? Is God truly dead? Or is it only a bad dream and nothing else? Will there return any Divine being any day again, who will take away the fears and the despairs of existence being swirled by this meaningless whirling of the storms of time?

In this book I have sought answers to these questions. The source of my knowledge has been me, who is bigger than the man, who is limited by the ego-bound will and the events of the world. There exists a "higher being" who has spoken within me. In this book I shall present a discourse that originates from this Being, who has guided me since my childhood.

I have received this vision of an enlightened world from this inner guide. The ideas of this enlightened world have been presented in another book titled "Vision of An Enlightened World (A Cosmic Perspective)". In the present book I shall delve with the questions of the nature of the will and the world, and the role that any higher being may play in our life, as well as explain how this inner being may be conceived and understood. I shall present these thoughts in the background of the social-political situations in the world today, while subjecting them to the knowledge of science and technology, which I have been able to acquire during my life. The content is divided into two parts: Part one mainly focuses on the nature of human will, which throws lights in the happenings of history since the beginning of civilization till today. It also discusses the basis of belief, moral, and values which have directed human behavior in building and sustaining social structure and interactions in different periods of history. The values of love, compassion, solidarity, empathy, dialogue and cooperations compared to competitions, greed, selfishness, exploitations, treachery, lie and unethical conducts to achieve success and power are subjects of discussed in the perspective of evolution and survival of the human specie. Rational explanations are sought in defining the issue of evil and good, the meaning of life and death, and distinguishing happiness and suffering of life. These values and visions are projected from the perspective of my understanding that the creation of the universe bears a meaning in all existence.

What is that meaning, and how life on Earth can attune itself to this meaning, and human beings may build a foundation of a new social-political order on the basis of this understanding has been the main purpose of my other book "Vision of An Enlightened World"[1], which complements the contents of this book.

In part two, more practical questions have been addressed, which may help the new generation to take actions and decisions as to how to react to the forces that may wish to mold their life and define its meaning. It will give them reflective insights into the way the will and world may encroach upon their personal territories and try to take hold of the destiny of their life in pathways which may be against the values and visions they do not desire. It is a guide for bringing change and building a new world where the higher-man may rise and triumph.

In the end of part II I have also added "GITA OF THE WILL AND THE WORLD," which I wrote about 17 years ago. The writing of this

---

1   For information visit http://BooksOfExistence.no

section, in a stark contrast with the intellectual analysis reflected in the rest of the writing, has risen through a mental process where intellectual interference on my side has been totally absent. During the writing of this section the ego-bound mind had not played any part. Instead, it was overwhelmed by a mental state, which one may call ghostly. This ghostly writer was outside the sphere of reasoning where the will-bound intellect conceives ideas and create thoughts. This abnormal writing had emerged while mind had submitted itself to a process in the brain, that I can not explain. It was like loosing oneself to a ghostly being, who has made use of the mind, which I call mine, to send the messages, which are not easy to decipher by using the intelligence and intellect I possess. However, I add it in this book to remind the readers that the same human existence is the origin of both mental processes - one is normal and driven by human intelligence and intellect, and the other is abnormal and driven by a ghostly power emerging through the mind. It has sometimes spoken as Man, sometimes as Man-God, and sometimes as God. All these are beyond comprehension by using normal way of thinking and arguing. If not they are any words of God, at least they reveal a peculiar aspect of activities of human brain.

Part I

SOCIETY MORALITY
BIOLOGY AND
COSMOS

WORLD AND WILL

In this chapter I shall describe the way I have understood the nature of the world and the emergence of will with which human specie act and decide in the world to give shape to the reality of life on Earth. By world I shall refer to the matter-based reality that impinges on the mind and creates the foundation of the will with which we operate and interact with the world. The experiences of the matter-based reality come to us through the sense apparatuses that we possess. Through seeing, hearing, touching, tasting, smelling and observing impacts of one thing onto another, which cause changes in the environment and the existing material set up, we realize the presence of the world around us. This perceptible world is divided into two categories: One without life and the other which possesses life, or constitutes the foundation of the process which we call life. The first is the physical inanimate world; the second is the biological world which bears the will in the world in the way we know it. However, these experiences of the world are confined within our home on Earth and its immediate planetary neighborhood. We assume that the world would reveal itself as experiences with similar attributes if we were transported into another part of the universe. In doing this we operate with certain ideas and concepts about the universe and its working methods, which are home grown and based on earthly experiences. The way we understand the universe and our position in it, colors the modality with which we operate. Our views about the cosmos impart on us the methods to observe and judge the conditions of our reality. So our view and understanding of the world are dependent on our concepts and knowledge about the universe. Without referring to the cosmos, where the reality of our experiences get its meaning and expressions through conscious reflections by the mind, the world would be devoid of meaning.

WORLD

The Physical World

What is this physical world made of? Though things in daily experiences make everything appear rudimentary and many may feel no need to delve into this question beyond using and utilizing the physical world according to needs, the question leads to a mind boggling arena, which will baffle and confuse even the most powerful human intellect. They are made of extremely tiny packets of energies arranged in an incredulously intelligent way. The packets are basically two types: They are called leptons and hadrons. One is light and the other is heavy. The hadrons can form a tight packets of many of its members, which thus form the nucleus of an atom, which draws the electron-leptons towards it and form the atoms. The bigger the number of hadrons in the nucleus the larger are the number of electrons which revolve around it. The weight of the nucleus decides the weight of the atom. Different nuclear sizes and electron configurations around them generate different atomic elements as we know them. The material world is made of these different atoms. However, the atoms are no big things: There are about 100 trillions of atoms in a size of an animal cell, which is about 10 microns in size.

When several atoms stick together they form molecules. The ways they form and break depend on the amount of energy required to bind the different parts together. In different conditions of temperature and pressure they can break and form and the molecules may arrange themselves in orderly or disorderly fashions. When the molecules do not cohere in an orderly fashion they form gaseous phase. When they fall into an orderly arrangement they assume solid character. In intermediate stage they behave like fluids. In conditions existing on the surface of the Earth, some elements exist as gas, some as liquid and some as solid; and some vary among all these three phases with changing conditions of heat and cold. How the molecules arrange under different pressures and temperatures decide the properties of matter- their visual appearance; sound, heat, electricity and light propagation

16

through them; their tolerance to external impact; their volatility, and ignition properties etc. These constant changes occurring all around cause the changing colors in the sky, form wind, rain and storm, bring ice and cold, sooth our bodies with breeze, sunshine and feelings of pleasure and warmth. The source of all these sentimental feelings is the mechanical motions of atoms and molecules constantly joining, falling apart and then forming new bonds with nature and making journey on Earth as atmosphere swinging with heat and cold, from night and day. During this dance of the molecules the energies are being released and absorbed, the radiations are being emitted and exchanged, the invisible laws of nature are conducting the symphony where all players must synchronize with the rhythm of the cosmos, to make it a reality that can sustain the marvel which we experience as our world.

Some movements and changes occur on daily basis, like winds changing directions and speed or intensity, the sun rays severing the cloud layers and breaking forth or the sunny sky suddenly getting covered by the layers of clouds bringing snow or rain; or the ripple gradually transforming into large waves carrying energies that can rock larger ships and boats to the point of falling into wrecks. The natural patterns of such changes are now understood from the laws of movements of things. They follow daily rhythms of rotation of Earth around itself, the attractions by the nearby moon, the streams and flows generated due to the drags and frictions and different pressure fronts circulating in the atmosphere etc. They are caused by natural order of things set in motions by the cosmic orbs and their arrangements in the cosmic arena that produce specific conditions of pressure, temperature and balance of forces which decide the way things flow, move or remain immobile. All movements are intricately balanced by all other movements caused by natural transformation of states of things that follow the lawful behavior of the clusters of molecules which hide the assembly of tiny energy packets.

The visible and the perceptible changes in the world appear different depending on the time scale in which the world is observed. Beyond the days the changes appear with seasons that affect the behavior of the living world while the temperature, pressure and energy input in the atmosphere from the sun vary with seasons. The cause of these changes can be attributed to the varying distance of the Earth from the Sun as it orbits around the star in a rhythmical cycle of one year. The living world on Earth changes its color and character with this cosmic movement. Though there is no God, everything seems destined by the cosmic happenings: Life follows death and death is followed by resurrection years after years. It is mechanical but complexly entangled with the existence of all in the cosmos. Any minutest disturbance in one place will disturb the pattern in which the reality is arranged all over the world.

If one looks at things in a higher time scale, the reality would look even more dramatically different than those brought by seasonal changes. Only a few millions of years ago no human beings existed on Earth. The climate was different; the mountains and lands were not there where they are now; the species inhabiting the Earth were different. If we go back in few hundred millions of years, there were no flowers and fruits, no plants and animals on land. Bacteria, protozoa and simple life forms in sea dominated the living arena of this planet. There were no intelligent creatures to ask about the deeper questions of life on Earth and existence of the universe.

One wonders what caused the appearance of life and why? Who are we? Why have we appeared on this planet? Is there any purpose and meaning behind our existence?

These are extremely difficult questions to answer. Before venturing into any effort, which may resemble like an answer, let me first describe the way I understand the existence of life i.e. the biological world.

The Biological World

The biological life is made of the same molecular elements which fill water and air of Earth. The same carbon, oxygen, hydrogen and nitrogen, which fill the atmosphere, assemble together to form the organic molecules, which are the basis of life. Two sorts of arrangements of these molecules - amino acids and nucleic acid -constitute the foundation of the biological world. They form the cells, which behave as living units that can divide and multiply by a mechanism inherent in their own structures. While 100 trillion atoms comprise a cell, a human body, for example, is comprised of nearly the same number of cells. So we are nothing but a packet of 10000 trillion trillions of atoms, which are built of energy packets of hadrons and electrons. But how could the molecules we find in the atmosphere turn into living creatures? There are many theories around this mystery: Some believe that the atmospheric conditions on Earth billions of years ago were ripe for the formation of the macro-molecules from which the DNA, RNA and amino acids evolved. This theory, in turn, hinges on the theory of formation of Earth from a molten ball of lava, which cooled and formed atmosphere around the planet. In the early days the atmosphere experienced violent conditions of electric discharge combined with extreme heat. It is argued that the molecules for building amino acids and nuclei acids came into existence at that time as results of the natural forces: In fact, the nature acted as the hands of God.

After different amino acids came into existence, they formed long chains. The sequence, in which the amino acids arranged themselves in chains, decided the types of jobs they were able to perform in the living world. These chains were called proteins. The different sequences of amino acids created different proteins, which were the power houses, where all activities of life were performed. From hundreds to thousands of amino acids formed a protein, where molecules were packed into three-dimensional shapes. First the chains either took the shape of helical springs, or folded ribbon like structures. Then these ribbons and springs twisted and turned to create three-dimensional geometric shapes. The way these folding occurred depended on the charge properties of the assembly of molecules contained in the chains and their reactions to temperature, pressure and acidity or alkalinity of the aqueous environment in which they grew.

The life first started in the water by following the acidity and alkalinity of the hydrological environment of Earth at that time. The air, the wind, the dancing waves all contributed in the chances of the molecules to adhere into proteins. Life emerged out of the cosmic symphony being played in the physical world.

Even more miraculous chains appeared as the nucleic acids. The De-oxyribonucleic acid (DNA), made of long double chains of molecules, contains codes of life. Each chain contained billions of molecules called bases which came in four types. Two chains were connected with each other by paring of bases: Base molecule from one chain associated with a base in the other chain. These base pairs formed the steps of a twisted helical ladder, known as double helix. The way the base pairs were arranged along the double helix decided the nature of life. They contained all the codes with which trillions of cells in the body were made. These codes decided the specie characteristics, individual physical appearance, life span, disease, mental abilities etc. The chains contained the codes in different segments, called genes. The total number of genes varied from different forms of life and specie to specie. The humans have about 20 000 genes. Some life form has more than 100 000. The genes contain the instructions about how the organelles in the new cells will be created, sustained and refurbished. The major activity is the fabrication of proteins. In creating a protein, a gene becomes active and the segment containing the gene untwines to give birth to a chain of molecules, called mRNA, which brings the code of life to a construction site in the cell, where the amino acids are spliced together and folded into a protein structure. Like this, everything belonging to the life process are made by following the codes imprinted in genes. While in the digital computers the coding is done with only 0 an 1, in the case of life it is done with four base molecules.

DNA, which contains all the genetic information of a life form, is a nanometer thin chain made of billions of base pairs. It remains packed inside the cell in a small area of a few microns (it is like packing one kilometer thread into a size of 1 mm). In humans when a cell divides in order to multiply, the DNA coils into 23 pairs of chromosomes (46 total). With cell division the 46 chromosomes create duplicate copies and then separates equally in two halves forming two cells with 46 chromosomes in each. The way the DNA duplication, and cell division occurs is mind boggling: It is difficult to grasp how the incredible and awesome program, which cause all these to occur with meticulous per-

20

fection as process of life, may have come into existence following the mechanical laws of nature.

There is a general consensus among the scientists that this has evolved through billions of years`trial and error by nature. Changing environments have set the molecules to assemble and form to fit into the best possible configuration that may survive the environmental stress and changes. They have been wafted by the air and the wind and agitated by cold and heat since the days of the formation of these chains of molecules, who have learnt to move by themselves without being carried by external agents. They have learnt to generate the energy and power from within themselves that may be used to transport them physically from one place to another. By this method, they have managed to survive by avoiding unfavorable environment and choosing physical conditions more amenable to the chance of survival. Easy access to amino acids with which the DNAs may manufacture proteins, have led them to prey on structures and life forms which are unable to defend themselves against more intelligent organisms. Life has thus evolved by preying on lesser intelligent creatures, who could not find ways to survive against the threats of the competitors. Thus the evolution of life has started from the cellular level of bacteria and viruses to the stage of the humans contain trillions and trillions of such cells.

According to this evolutionary theory of life the genes have learnt to modify themselves in order to remain effective in reproducing and transcribing life which would be more adaptable to the availability of food and surrounding physical conditions. Thus life forms have diversified and spread to fit into different circumstances existing on the surface of the Earth. More and more complex organisms have evolved with the passage of time. With the passing of time more and more intelligence were required to survive the competitions for resources needed to feed millions and millions of species of living creatures who filled the biosphere of the planet.

The humans descended after evolution passed through many stages. A branch of the reptiles evolved into mammals. A branch of the mammals, in turn, evolved into apes. The humans descended from these apes. The way it has come about has environmental reason, as well the intelligence to secure and protect oneself against the predators, and strategy to overcome the enemies and overwhelm the creatures who were preyed on. It has involved cooperation among the individual members of the specie and their joint efforts to seek a common goal, as well as loyalty, dexterity and adherence to some common norms, principles and values which forged cooperation among the group.

WILL

In the Physical World

Will can be defined as a power inherent in an object with which it re-sponds and interacts with the world which surrounds it. In that sense all hadrons and electrons possess will, by which they form bonds with other members of the same group, or with the other group of energy packets. The way this associations happen and the resulting object of the association characterize the nature of the will. Hadron form tiny packets of atomic nuclei, as well as possess charges with which they establish bonds with electrons. The way they associate or dissociate with the other objects in the world bring the effects of the will in the world and build the foundation of the existence of the world. The nu-clear binding between protons and neutron, and electromagnetic force between a proton and an electron define the will of the protons to as-sociate itself with others in the world. Similarly atoms form associa-tions with other atoms building the content of the material substances that we know. The molecules cluster to form the basic building blocks of life, which in turn cluster in millions or hundreds of millions to form the proteins and DNAs. On may argue that this will is mechani-cal and fixed, determined by the charge content and arrangements of the atoms and molecules. It behaves according to the charge distribu-tion and its strength. It has no will to defy the modes in which similar objects should interact with the surrounding reality of the world. It only reacts to the presence of the world and seeks its own position in the world in the stream of movements of things undergoing constant transitory changes. In that sense will is the foundation of the world; while the world, in which the will remains immersed, gives will its appearance and form. By binding and associating with the world the will manifests. The charges manifest as the expression of the will as the world takes its physical form through attractions and repulsions. This will is not free. The content of the world and movements in which the objects in the world are set, condition the way the interacting object finds its destiny in the world. In no way it can free itself or choose the conditions in which it wishes to fulfill its destiny.

In the living world

The higher forms of life are characterized by the possibility of choices i.e. the freedom to move away or towards environments in which it may discover different possibilities of interacting with the world. This choice of associating or dissociating with particular given conditions is the sign of freedom, which characterizes higher will that is manifest in the living world. Freedom is a way to leave behind a given condition and seek a new foundation of life in the world. However, the degrees of freedom vary with the number of possible conditions one may choose from. At primary level the freedom is conditioned by necessities. Life always moves to environments where it may find more food and face less threat to its existence created by adverse environment. It always seeks its destiny where there are less predators and less competitions for satisfying the needs. This form of will, which chooses with freedom and associates or dissociates with an environment and acts to seek newer grounds for its existence on own initiative, characterizes the will of the living world. To express this will the creatures develop physical mechanism to react, respond, attach or withdraw from another existence and the surrounding. They develop nerves that carry the messages about the conditions throughout the living body so that the body can activate the mechanisms to choose, respond and act accordingly. In a higher manifestation of this will, the signals are organized, stored as memories, information is retrieved when necessary and analyzed to decide the way to respond and act with respect to a situation. At this stage of development, brain and a central nervous system forms, and intelligence appears in the way of brain activities. Though the neurons, which conduct information from brain to all other parts of the body, still make use of the physical laws of conduction of the ionic charges through material substrata comprising the body, at this level the will appears free from the physical laws: It is not the physical laws which blindly dictate the way to response to the world, but another dimension of life gets added to the world of charges and currents.

The capacity to make use of the information, retrieve data from memory and make judgements about the nature of the situation on the basis of what has been experienced and learnt from earlier circumstances, and then decide about the best way to act and respond in order to achieve the desired circumstance of life, is the foundation of the free will. The will to survive by overcoming the challenges of the world is the primary nature of this free will. Without this will the living creatures will be prey of circumstances, and loose the power to survive. One may also see it in another way: In the form of a will to dominate and subjugate the weaker creatures, who one may encounter in the way of struggle for survival. By restricting and depriving others of freedom and possibilities, one seeks to enhance one`s own with the aim to secure one`s conditions of survival. One uses knowledge, intelligence and strategy to make it a success. The better the capacity of the brain, more advantage one enjoys with this free will.

The will to live and the will to overwhelm and subjugate the weaker ones is common among all animals, including the humans. It is an expression of freedom and security to exploit arenas of life where one may strive and grow easily at the expense of the others. However, this will is imposed by the world: The conditions and circumstances of the world put animals in competitions and struggle for survival. Without willing to defend one`s interest one may perish. So will acts as mechanisms of defense and security against the predators, who roam all around, wherever life has expressed itself with its will to live. Major part of the animal activities are driven by this will. There exists no respite from it.

While the will to live reflects the nature of the living world, where everybody is busy in securing their grounds for existence, there exists other dimensions of will in the world, which are free from the necessities of physical survival.

Will is an expression of the presence of intelligence in the world through the neuronal network of the brain. More evolved brain is the sign of more intelligence - the expression of the living world to transcend the limitations and conditioned imposed by the physical laws. The intelligence brings the knowledge and understanding of the laws and how to make use of this knowledge in transforming and manipulating the physical world in one`s favor. It creates new grounds bringing new relations of things with themselves and the human will. By knowing how to enhance the possibilities of growth by creating new conditions of one`s own innovation, the human will is able to redefine the premise of its existence in an innovative way. Thus it makes itself free from the dictates of the physical world and the blind will moving as the material content of the world. This power depends on the development of the brain and the genetic basis on which the life is coded. The more one may use this capacity, the codes may mutate and generate greater possibilities to achieve this power to transcend the blind path of the will. Thus will is something that evolves and emerges with the evolution of life as expressions of the intelligence that permeates all existence. However, the intelligence is something that needs a computer to be programmed. The neuronal network in the brain provides the computer. Without it intelligence finds no expression in the world. Life forms without possessing brains are thrown into the blind alleys of the will that can not be freed from the laws of nature and the events churning in the universe in a mechanical way.

Though world is the foundation of the will, like the network of the brain, communicating by electrical signals and chemical secretions through an entangled pathways of hundreds of billions of neurons, the will evolves as something that can redefine the world and set new dimensions to the existence of the matter-bound reality. Through the manifestation of the will, corroborated with intelligence, the world receives a dimension which we may call non-material or spiritual. The material world hides the existence of the spiritual essence of existence, which only comes to expression through higher evolution of the brain.

The will is the essence of our mind, a spiritual reality which emerges through the working of our brains. Like a charge is embedded in a hadron or an electron, this spiritual essence envelopes the living world, which we experience as the existence of mind. It is the foundation of the psyche based on the soma. By controlling and regulating the somatic activities we can penetrate into the mystery of this psychic dimension; similarly by unfurling the psychic power we can generate new foundations of somatic existence. Through the body mind manifests; similarly mind is the one which seeks the best opportunities for the fulfillment of the needs of the body in the worldly arena, and imparts on the world changes in order to restructure it to fulfill its freedom.

So the will is not confined to the physical laws, though ionic activities of the neurons constitute the worldly foundation of the way the mind manifest through the activities of the brain. Only in complex organizations of matter as in a brain the will manifests as the essence of the living world.

Will is borne by the matter in the brain and the neuronal circuits and constantly affected by the sensations and signals, which impact the material foundation of the mind. With the world moving around, and events passing by, while churning the senses, the will flows as streams of thoughts seeking modes of response to the outside world which demands actions and attentions from the mind. The will has the power to disentangle itself from the happenings in the world and negate the demands of the physical world, arriving as sensations and feelings and generating thoughts. It can choose to process the neuronal activities in a way that is dependent on the will and not on the happenings in the world. It can take control of how the world will be received by the responses by the brain, and thus posit the existence outside the material conditioning of the world. It can transcend the world and make the world effectively non-existing with respect to the mental activities. This is the meditative power of the will, that can turn the world into a void in terms of response from the will-bound mind. By this meditating power the mind can penetrate into the mystery of the will that emerges by using matter of the world as vehicles, but is not one with it. By this way the mind can experience the aspect of existence which exists in the state of the void, i.e. no world and nothing. This is the

26

highest source of power that animate the living process and its will to engage or not to engage in the world as expression of freedom, which reflects the spiritual nature of existence.

Like the power of the will which can stop the flow of thoughts and events in the mind, as if the world surrounding the body has disappeared and non-existent, it can also simulate events, thoughts and feelings, which would have appeared in the mind if the world was framed with certain conditions of existence. It can make a non-existing world appear in thoughts, which can generate brain activities similar to the effects a real world would create. In that way, will can create the experiences of a situation, which may not be happening in reality. In that way it can create the world as a phenomenon of the mind

This power of the will can also mirror the experiences of other beings. It can experience the mental states of the others caught in a condition of the world by mirroring the neuronal events that would have been created if one was amidst such situation. This gives the will the power to feel the pain, suffering and joy of the fellow beings. This is a way to feel one with others. It lies at the root of compassion and altruistic values. More evolved a mind, more abilities one develops to erase the presence of the world, or mirror the world that others may be experiencing, in order to establish the power of the mind over the physical conditions of the world. In contrast, in less evolved beings the world controls the will instead, and guides it in blind alleys, where one experiences narrow paths of freedom.

WILL AND SOCIAL EVOLUTION

My main starting point of discussion about the nature of will, and the way it affects the social development, will be the DNA codes of life.

The chains of billions of base pair molecules contain programs to reproduce exact copy of itself by dividing and then forming the nuclei of new cells. The DNA codes decide the way the brain structure and neuronal network forms and thus gives rise to the intelligence, which governs the methods of adaptation with the conditions of the world.

The primary function of this will is to reproduce life in the world and run the program encoded in the base pairs inside DNA, which control functional characteristics of life including aging and dying. It runs the program and brings the steps of life in its course and then resets the cycle again for the next generation. The program takes into account the changing and fluctuating conditions of the world, which move and remain animated all the time as results of the dance of water and air, and caused by the scarcity or abundance of supply of molecules needed to sustain the physicochemical processes. The parts of the brain structure, which we have inherited from primitive animals as results of evolutions, provides automatic responses and reaction methods to the changing world, like intake of food and drink, and warning against threats and dangers to life. More advance part of the brain generates emotions and feelings, which are not automated responses like primitive instincts, but methods of gauging and deciding the response needed in a given situation in order to succeed in resolving challenges of the world. Anger, hate, jealousy, depression etc. are some modes which create a negative response to the world and inspire man to withdraw from the situation and seek new relations. Similarly love, joy and happiness are positive modes, that inspire man to relate to the world and fulfill the possibilities of life. Through emotional reactions one detaches, or attaches oneself to the given conditions of the world, where one may find oneself. Primarily the genes seek ground where there are plenty of food needed for survival, or there are ways to manufacture the needed nutritions from the substances present in the surrounding. Where there exist scarcity, the life moves away from that environment. Apart from the food supply, the climate and hazards, which may threaten the existence of life, play decisive roles in the pursuit of animals in seeking secure arena, where one may reproduce. In many situations the animals move from one place to another in search for the optimal world for survival. The need for survival and functioning of the genetic mechanisms of reproduction and continuation of the species, is the most central aspect of the will in the world. In some cases the genes may mutate in order to re-encode itself that may increase the chance of its reproductive success in the given environment. So the genes are not any inflexible coded program, but contain flexible methods of adaptation by changing the codes in which life may survive in a given environment. It can both respond to an environment with positive or negative emotions, and distance or attach itself, or may mutate to fit into the given world that may increase its potential of growth. This intelligence is characteristic of life forms, which define the fundamental nature of the will.

With higher form, i.e. with more evolved brain, containing complex neuronal functions, coordination and communications among different parts of the brain, the intelligence also shows up in the form of cooperation and sharing among the members of the specie. In a world infested with predators all around, where everybody is seeking its most favorable ground for survival and feeding arena, for continuing its reproductive cycle, the world turns very competitive. Intelligence leads man to take advantage of the kinship and friendship relations, while one expects more willingness to share and cooperate among kin and friends than in the others living in the larger world where everybody is thrown into competition with everybody.

This organization, which brings advantage of survival, among family members and friends, is the first social unit, which brings values outside the competition into the social fabrics built on human interactions. It brings the value of reciprocating favors and help at the moment of one`s need by doing the same when the other may fall into a similar situation. It acts as a valve to safeguard oneself from unpredictable moments of needs and necessities of life. In human sphere, besides the material needs, it includes a more advanced form of conduct, like sharing the psychological distress. However, they are often geared to support a narrow band of human relationships, motivated by the interests of the social unit to which one belongs..Thus this kind of higher values, that help to coherer and cooperate, may also prove to be more conducive for survival.

When such family and kinship units adhere together to form a greater social structure, new forms of social rules develop. Most often these larger organization takes place with the aim of gaining benefits from each others, and making life more easy to live and reproduce by sharing labour, resource and knowledge. In a community it becomes much easier to maintain the reproductive cycle, although the pressure to share the resources among more people may add to more scarcity and challenges to meet the daily needs. However, in a society with more diversification of skill, the social structures add to diversification of products and thus more possibilities of exchange of products and development of a market. Exchange of products is an intelligent way of resolving the needs and substituting one particular need by an alternative method.

At this level, where social structure gives birth to a market, the values take a new definition. One talks about material value and the psychological value. Material value relates to what material good one may get by exchanging a product one produces; the psychological value is how the service done to someone brings comforts and positive emotions among the members of the society and to oneself. The psychological value is measured in terms of increasing the social sentiments of sharing and cooperating at the emotional level, which may bring a sense of added security to the group.

The will to belong to a group, which can provide a sense of material and psychological security is very fundamental in the social cohesion. Therefore socialization and social identity becomes important in the animal world. Socialization functions around some social norms and values,which all members are expected to follow. The strength of the cohesive power of these norms and values to keep the individuals attached to the social fabric depends on the material and psychological securities and advantage the members may enjoy. The psychology of fear has also been an element in sewing the social fabric together: First the fear of the social authority holding power in deciding the norms and values, and then the fear of heaven and unseen world, like spirits, ghosts, devils, angels and gods.

The psychology of fear has been an important instrument in weaving a social bond. The fear of authority, who can inflict punishment for breaking the social norms, has been central in most social systems. In many social structures these fears have been inbred in the name of the invisible powers acting behind the scenes. Through the representations of mythological animals and symbols these fears are intensified in the psyche of the social creatures and given religious meanings. Thus religions become crucial in forging and upholding social norms and values under the power of an unseen authority, which could not be challenged by the earthly inhabitants.

One may wonder how genes benefit from such a method of creating spectre of fear by projecting imaginary ideas, which have no reality in the world? Why do genes create heaven, when world is the only physical basis of its existence? Why it assumes the existence of a non-existent world where unworldly creatures who have no genetic counterparts are projected to exist? Why genes adopt such mechanism of controlling the behavior of the human beings, whose life is solely steered by the programs encoded in the genes? Is it an evolutionary tactic to create a fear based on non-existing beings in order to control what exist?

Anyway, it is a reality of the human society that there exists a fear about the existence of an unseen world, which is beyond the realm of perceptions and the capacity of knowing by man. It castes its influence over worldly matters of life, whose source is the human will. These fears are often exploited by some individuals to gain own advantage. One may argue that it is an innovative idea of some intelligent human beings to invent heaven, and the unseen worlds where the powerful beings may exist. This can be seen as a smart way for these intelligent individuals to caste their influence and power over the society. It can be a tactic of the smarter people to take control over the others in order to secure evolutionary advantage over the other members of the group. Such fears rooted in religious belief and existence of heaven and hell have been very effective in controlling the mass.

In many societies the individuals, who claimed relationships or contacts with the unknown supernatural world, won favour and were accepted as authority of power. They inculcated the belief in the population that the problems of the earthly life could only be ameliorated with the help of the divine grace. This tactic has dominated the human society from the time of early civilization we know of.

After building religious institutions there was a need to protect the system from attacks by unfriendly groups, who, in search of power may feed other religious belief in the society. It brought the "social genes" to activate the mechanisms of defense against intrusions and occupations by foreign communities. Mighty men and soldiers emerged to defend the social structures - in a way similar to the mechanism of defense by the biological cells. They secured the institutions against the attackers. Their success or failure decided their ranks in the social power hierarchy. The authority, dealing with the divine grace and having control over the population, often parcelled the power to the soldiers, who could successfully defend the institutions and resources. In a more elaborate social organization, like in a state, they finally were elevated as the kingly men, who in alliance with the religious priesthood kept their sway of power over the rest of the population.

The position of power in a society always brought favorable access to material resources and manpower, with which one could easily boost one's level of comforts and extravagance, and reduce enemies, who may like to rise in challenging the system. With power in hands, one could easily build alliances with other individuals by disbursing rights to property, wealth and ranks in exchange of loyalty and support. Thus a smaller group, within a larger social group, fed on the weaker members. We know how it functioned only a century ago in the feudal structures (which exist even toady in some places).

Some argue that this desire to come to power and dominate over the fellow beings, who are weaker, is natural in the gene of the animals, including the human. Sharing the prosperity and security of life with others occur only when it deems advantageous to one's own interest and further enhancement of strength and security against the challenges from the competitors.

In a more stable society, where conflicts of power is less pronounced, and there exists a better consensus about the way power should be managed and population should be controlled, so that positive feelings of happiness and peace may prevail among all, new social values emerge. Compassion for the weak develops. In the beginning it may start with self-interest, like preserving the security of survival for the members of one's own family, who may not be robust enough to compete and survive on one's own. The interest to secure the life of the closer kin, who may be weak, brings demands of solidarity in the society for the weaker ones. This generates new values outside the "Darwinian killing field" where treachery, lechery and whatever may bring success are considered as the allowed and viable methods for anyone, who can flex strength. When members of own family becomes beneficiaries of this value of compassion, one easily accepts the rights of the others to enjoy the same. Competitions give way to cooperation and sharing. However, it only happens in a society where there exists abundance of resources and enough safety of life for all in an environment which is not churned by intense conflicts and brutal power struggle.

The above conjecture is based on the proposition that values of compassion is not compatible with the social development where scarcity and necessity are dominant factors. Compassion takes roots in a society where people enjoy positive emotions in their environment and social interactions. The prerequisite for these values to evolve is peace, or less tensions as regards the distribution of power and social goods.

One also sees compassion and sacrifice in situations of need where poverty may reign. One may wonder, is it then against the natural behavior, as the Darwinian have prescribed? I believe love, which creates attraction and attachment, which one does not want to depart with at any cost, can generate such behavior. In exceptional cases, a higher aspect of the human mind shines forth, which generate altruism and sacrifice of one`s life for the benefit of the other human beings. One may define this higher love as a sentiment that puts the value of life of the beloved as same, or higher than oneself, which inspires one to sacrifice one`s life to preserve the life of other. But how should one understand this sacrifice from the biological point of view? By activating the sentiment of such love what does one wish to attain in the evolutionary process?

However, to suffer for the happiness of others is a rare case. Most natural is to make others suffer for one`s own happiness. Exploitations and living on others`labour and toil at the expense of others`security are the normal way of life. It is biologically more natural as species have learnt to fight and win by subjugating other species and dominating over them. Whenever there are suitable opportunities, this behavior continues within the members of the same specie. The smart and intelligent members find ways to control the social system in their favour so that such exploitation may be realized and sustained. It is done through building institutional structures around the economic activities, and distributing the power of authority in controlling the social behavior through cultural and religious norms. The information and knowledge that can be vital in winning over the enemies, and suppress any social revolt, remain closed secrets for those who form the power elites of the society. To facilitate this process of domination, armed organs are maintained, who protect the established institutional order.

Like climatic changes, social climates also change with the spread of information and knowledge, and increased insight into the dynamics of the social process - the way they are controlled and governed. Newer discoveries about the nature of the world, civilization and cultures and possibilities of newer methods of exploring resources and accumulating wealths have changed social climates many times before with the passage of history. Knowledge about the working of the nature and the intelligence to make use of the knowledge in strengthening one`s military capacity to capture territories and markets outside one`s own, have vastly changed the course of history during the last few hundred years. For example, the traditional mechanism, which held its grip for a long time, as feudal-oligarchical social system allied with the priesthood, had faced challenges after the scientific knowledge, and information about the greater world became known.

The scientific knowledge brought new social actors into play, who could make use of the discoveries in making life easier to live for the people. The chances of survival by increased output with less expense of labour and facilities of communication by mechanized means, greatly changed the social reality. With it the genes became more adaptive to this new condition and found it a more suitable ground to breed. So the alliance and loyalty with the tradition actors dwindled, and the new class bearing the knowledge of the scientific world gained more and more preponderance and authority. It was like moving into a new environment more suitable for survival. Though the physical framework remained intact, the relationship with the physical world drastically altered. So knowledge became the new ground to seek success and dominance over the less fortunate ones.

How did one get this knowledge? Who had implanted the program in the genes that could decipher the codes (or laws) that run the physical world? How could the great mystery of nature came to light? Were they revealed by the mysterious grace of God, or did they appear as accidental crossing of phenomena revealing the relationships hidden among things that unlocked the codes as thoughts and ideas in the mind? How could intelligence, coded by the genes, unlock the mystery of the laws of nature, which, in its turn, had brought the formation and existence of genes?

This power of the scientific mind became the builder of the new society. Mind was no more the passive receptor of the world, unknown and mysterious, which moved and animated the will into actions. The knowledge about the mystery behind the working of the world transformed the social structure in favour of the men of science. The authority of power, which the priests and the oligarchs enjoyed before, moved now in the hands of those who sowed the seeds of knowledge. It brought the age of scientific enlightenment. The traditional mechanism of keeping people ignorant and fearful of the power of heaven, which helped to control and exploit the mass in the society, came under challenge. More heaven fell and people understood about science, more their alliances shifted from the traditional power elite to the new emerging power structure. The scientific discoveries also followed new methods of deciding values of goods and labour, and new mechanisms of exchanging goods in the market were introduced. The idea of the paper money came to take over the valuation of things in the market. With it, the bankers and the banking system spread, which controlled the way the money was managed, and flowed in the market. The knowledge of science, and this innovative strategy of controlling the values in the market by using money brought those with smarter genes, fit to operate in this new environment to replace the old power structure. With money one could buy labour and employ people in productions that were more efficient, as results of application of scientific methods. It generated more revenues in the market. These smarter men, found ingenious ways to generate money from "nothing" by introducing the ideas of making profits and reinvesting the profits in the production and valuing the products in ways that would bring even more profits. The method to multiply the profits and generate new money became the way of these new elites to take control of the economic power of the society.

The euphoria of this scientific age, introducing new values and efficient mechanisms of productions, and creating jobs for those, who needed

37

some means of economic survival, brought a social revolution. The allegiances of the mass switched to those who offered a better prospect of making a living. To attract the population to side with the new elites of industrial entrepreneurs, bankers and new market mechanisms, the traditional values pivoted on moral and values, propagated in the name of heaven and religion, were replaced by ideas that emphasized on the worth of the human endeavours and values of human liberty. These new ideological movement easily attracted the mass, which remained oppressed and exploited under the feudal system. The disadvantaged in the society could not be kept in servility anymore with the help of the traditional fear and the oppression by the feudal oligarchs. It gave rise to a history of revolution in modern time.

The ideas of liberty and freedom, supported by new production mechanisms and opportunities of employment, which strengthened the possibilities of survival and economic security, became the slogans of the new society and became the foundation of social ethics in modern time. The slogan was to free the oppressed from the chains. Those, who had no voice in the old society, where the powers to decide over the economy were totally monopolized by a few, were given the rights to participate in the social decision making. Thus democracy took its roots. It became an Enlightened Age guided by the men of science and reason.

The success in the world, where smarter functioning of certain genes once gave success in forming social-economic organization and brought advantage in manipulating and controlling the fellow human beings with strategies and tactics of exploitations, were now replaced by other genes i.e. those who create smarter reasoning and the capacity of the brain to analyses the world in a scientific manner. With the success of the reasoning brain the society and history totally transformed. With it, new values emerged, new relations among human beings were established, and new methods of control and manipulation and stabilizing the social dynamics evolved. So success of particular genes had made a havoc in the social structure and reorganized the human activities in a totally new path.

The nature of our will is influenced by the environment in the world where we live in. The ways we receive the benefits and services from the society, and get help in maintaining our daily livelihood and security, decide the way we activate our will in pursuit of changing, or submitting to the conditions of the world. Every society develops mechanisms to constrain freedom of such actions in order to stabilize certain values and mechanisms of functioning of the society, so that it does not slide into a chaos. These control are put in place by using some ideas about the nature of the world and ourselves, which would be best befitting the needs of those who govern and control the system.

In the new world, the freedom from oppression by the landowning class in the feudal structure, took another form of servitude. The bonanza of profits that the new world generated for the bankers and businessmen increased the lust for money, which could be easily generated by using the profits in successive turns. It became known as capitalism. The people owing money invested in the means of productions in order to make more profits and thus lived luxuriously without any need to work. Those, who were not fortunate like this moneyed class, had no other asset but their labor to sell in order to earn money to survive. The freedom in the new world became synonymous with the freedom of those who could invest money in order to exploit labor of those who owned nothing. The new social organization, built to support the ideas of capitalism, became a prison for the working class, who moved away from agriculture to industry.

The magic of creating money and prosperity by simply investing accumulated money and letting others work for the investor, became the foundation of exploitations in the capitalist world. The smarter genes found their ways in exploiting the new ideology in order to establish their hegemony in the social control.

A group of intellectuals, forming the middle-class, who were a by-product of the revolution that freed the society from the feudal oligarchs, and placed the power in the hands of the bankers, industrialists and traders instead, became the bearer of the lights of freedom. While freedom became a way for the capitalists to exploit freely the laboring class, the middle class intellectuals, inspired by the ideas of humanism, wished to free the society from the influence of the human genes prone to exploitation.

By then the education have spread among a wider section of the population with the establishments of higher institutions of learning; knowledge of science and philosophy and the ideas from other cultures of the world have already cast deep influences on the ways of thinking of people, whose worlds were previously circumscribed by ignorance and religious indoctrinations. The part of this educated class, who came from the backgrounds of families of teachers, lawyers, petty officials etc., forming a group between the moneyed class and the working labor class, became the bearer of conscience of humanity. They wished to free the history from the exploitations and injustice by a few over the rest of the society.

With the rise of science and the importance of knowledge, these intellectuals gave more attention in changing social structures by using the intellectual power of the mind: They sought scientific reasons behind the way history has evolved and social dynamics have changed the life of people in the world. They analyzed the way the social dynamics was moving, and how it could be given directions with the help of scientific knowledge and application of reason. They tried to find a theory of history and aspired to predict its course in the future, like a subject of physical science, where phenomena could be predicted for the future once the laws of nature were known and the initial data were available. With such models the rise of capitalism and its collapse in the future was predicted as inevitable laws of social science.

Now the genes were more geared to consider the effects of human endeavors than any heavenly, or other worldly interventions. The belief that everything rested in the human hands and the capacity of the human brain to penetrate into the working mechanism of the world including the development of history, became strong among these radical intellectuals. Will was reduced to the movement of events in the world and the inevitable laws which moved it to the destined direction. With a desire and ambition to decipher the laws of history they speculated about the way it may happen. Keeping faith in this model they wished to facilitate the occurrence of events that would establish the birth of the envisioned world sooner than at natural historic pace. Of course, there was no God in this picture of the world! Man was the maker of history and intellectual power of the mind had the ability to hasten and materialize the events of history, which follow lawful paths. Anyway, it was what the intellectuals, who challenged capitalism, believed. They were known as Marxists.

These leftist radicals believed that the exploitations of the labor by the capitalists will bring the collapse of capitalism as inevitable rise of the workers' revolt and the establishment socialism. The greed for profits will give rise to overproduction, which can not be absorbed by the market. It will result in the crisis of falling production and increasing unemployment, which will generate revolt among the workers already alienated by exploitations. With the collapse of capitalism the ownership of the means of production will be taken over by the society, who, instead of exploiting the workers, will pay them the just wages that they rightfully deserve.

The capitalistic competitions gave rise to two world wars during the first half of the twentieth century. After that the world had seen the rise and fall of Marxism and Socialism during the last fifty/sixty years. The rise of socialism and communism, however, did not follow the prescription of the Marxist theorists. They came as the world wars paved the way of dismantling the existing social systems by armed revolts. Instead of crisis of capitalism, they took place in a social setup where capitalism had not evolved to any substantial degree. Russia was more in their feudal structure and capitalism was in its infancy when the socialists revolutions swept the country. In China it came as an armed peasant revolution against a corrupt landowning class. However, the idea of the common ownership of land as well as economic means of productions came into vogue in the socialist/communist states, who defended their ideologies by using power and force. People were given the basic amenities of living and protection against capitalist exploitations, at the cost of freedom of religious belief, cultural practices, and pursuing personal greed for economic and social advantage. Things

41

had to be regimented and controlled down to the grass root level in order to implement the ideas of socialism into actions. Policing, spying and abuse of power by the cadres of the party, overlooking the functioning and implementation of the system, became the evil of the society.

Without private ownership rights people became reluctant to give their best efforts to produce for the common good. The power handed over to the party cadres became oppressive to the liberal minded and free thinking intellectuals, who were not convinced about the Marxist theory of history and social development. The fear of reprisal by the authority against those who criticized the system stifled the growth of social dynamics, while people could not feel free to talk and express opinions. While the wealthier and the educated class suffered maximum disadvantages in this socialist system, the workers got more to say in the way the economy should grow and prosper. The lack of intellectual resources and innovation among the workers, faced with isolations from the capitalist markets and their technological know-how, made the system untenable in the long run.

At the same time the power of the media and communication had been spreading in the world and becoming more and more advanced in penetrating into the socialist world, which tried to protect itself from the capitalist propaganda by censoring the information from outside. The rising consumer goods of luxury in the capitalist countries, while the department stores in the socialist countries remained empty, disillusioned the mass about the worth of choosing the socialist ideology. They opted for some sort of capitalism again. After experimenting with socialist ideas for a few decades, Russia and China both turned to pursue economic tracks in line with capitalism.

What does this social evolution really say about the human nature?

The human nature is not restricted to one type or a few characteristics, though there exists higher frequency for some traits to repeat in many. They can be environment dependent and conditioned by the social structures, rather than some behavior inherent in the genetic codes of the human specie.

Like all animals, human beings also respond to the environmental conditions and chooses modes of behaviors in order to adapt to the environment either by increasing or decreasing efficiency of the particular type of brain activities which can help to adjust with the surrounding, or by using intelligent innovative methods to affect and change the condition with the help of knowledge and experiences: Either one remolds oneself to the need of the world, or tries to remold the world to resolve the problems of necessity. Those members of the specie, who are more adaptive or innovative, enjoy more success in the society. It is a natural way the world and the will interact and contribute to the evolution.

The capacities of the individual brains vary, conditioned by the surrounding environment and the stimuli one receives from the world, as well as the genetic inheritance. The way one responds and tries to remold oneself or the world defines the smartness, or weakness of the person. Those, who succeed to resolve the problems of life in an efficient and risk free manner are considered to be more intelligent.

Normally there is a large variation of intelligences among the members of the society, which naturally results in large variations of capacities to respond to and modify the world, or oneself, according to the demands of existence. This variations emerge in the form of different traits of human characters: Some can be intelligent as regards using the reasoning part of the brain; some can show intelligence as regards creative thinking and imagination; some may show intelligence in economic speculations and manipulations which may bring successful results etc.

A society is a collection of all sorts of creatures and to define their common character can be hard except pointing to those that are most obvious in the animal world, to which the humans belong. These obvious elements are search for food, mate and a suitable environment for reproduction, secure and protect oneself and one`s progenies against the threatening forces of nature and the predators sprawling around, and define a safe territory of activities where the security of life may be more guaranteed. Many may be happy if these basic needs are met. However the most intelligent among them may strive to improve the set of conditions in which life must operate. They find innovative methods to make use of the existing elements in the world to form new relationships with nature that may bring more security and better guarantee for survival. More intelligent the individual more possibilities one may discover. This becomes the foundation of freedom.

Those who are unaware of the possibilities, and unable to make use of it, may like to submit to the primary needs of life and adapt to it. They may not feel any drive for freedom outside these basic satisfactions. However, the smarter and more intelligent ones remain hungry after looking for better possibilities to extend one`s territories of activities and gaining a better control of the situations of life: Without submitting to what seems to be the given condition in the world, they strive to recondition the world and establish new opportunities to extend one`s influence in the world. This becomes the ground for freedom that arises from the desire to seek a more fortunate state where life may unfold a greater perspective beyond eating, mating, working and fighting against the enemies and the predators.

If one trades in the area where there are several other intelligent people who are seeking the similar goal, the competitions will ensue. Competitions for more freedom and extended territories of human activities, which reflect the freedom of the mind to go beyond the blind conditions of the world, is more common with more intelligent people. One may call this as a higher nature of man i.e. to seek knowledge, use innovation and redefine the conditions of the world to reflect one`s freedom as a being who is not a slave of the environment.

In some cases this freedom, enacted by the more intelligent people, can be detrimental to the conditions of survival for the others, who are satisfied with the primary needs being met. The intelligent members may take the advantage of the ignorance and lesser security enjoyed by the others, and make use of the labors of the ignorant mass as the stepping stones for extending their freedom and power. However, a truly higher man does not take any comfort in exploiting anyone for the purpose of enjoying more freedom and comforts for oneself. The higher nature of man is not only to seek freedom through knowledge and creativity by keeping the power of the will at the focus of the world, but also to secure the life of fellow beings and enlighten them. The higher man teaches the fellow human beings how to follow the paths of freedom and emancipation from the bondage of the law-bound world.

The higher man sees the necessity of the others too to evolve and feel free and secure, as one may wish for the members of one`s own family and kin. He/she thinks about the security and freedom of all, and not for some at the expense of the rest. The ideas of Marx about the way the history may evolve following the dynamics of the material world and its contradiction may not be right, but his dream of a social order where all may feel secure and find meaningful way to live without being exploited by a few, points to the vision of a higher human society.

The socialism have failed to succeed as a viable social order because most societies are a mixture of individuals enjoying different levels of knowledge, information and awareness about the world and oneself. Most are still bound to the level that the satisfactions of basic securities can bring and whose compassion and concern for others do not go beyond the boundary of family and kinship. For most, the idea of love revolves around sexual attraction and parental attachment and not universal love that requires sacrifice for other human beings.

In the socialist movement, which focused on the ownership and management of the means of production by the workers and the rights of the workers to choose the proper labour conditions and facilities, the production mechanism lost the power of the will to innovate and be effective. The management suffered from party-political doctrines based on social theories rather than the given nature of the society and the human beings comprising the society. The curtailing of freedom of the people, who were more innovative, intelligent and seeking personal fulfillment of life, made the society economically stagnant. It mechanically produced the basic goods by regimented efforts of those who were indoctrinated in the ideology. There was a cry for freedom from thinkers, writers, artists and other intellectual communities.

The party political machinery became oppressive and authoritarian, and alienated the forces of freedom which are the main pillars of any healthy social growth. Instead of feeling brotherhood and common security, which everybody could trust without being discriminated for ideological and religious reason, there was an atmosphere of fear for those who differed with the ideology and carried religious beliefs. The social experiment of scientific materialism in human sphere, where life is incredibly complex with its innumerable emotional variations, was bound to fail.

Through use of knowledge about the way social-dynamics can be changed by the use of intelligence and the power of restructuring relationships with the living and non-living worlds, one may envisage different forms of social-order. One needs to make an intelligent choice among the possible models to further the advancement of the human civilization from here. Is there a direction that would be more befitting with reason?

The main reason could be the continuation of life on Earth and the evolution of man to a higher stage? So the choice of the social developments should be such that the human actions do not jeopardize the fine balance that exists between life and the physical environment of the world. The climate on Earth, and its diverse life forms - from bacteria to human being - are all intricately entangled and dependent on each other. Human actions may bring changes which may either turn devastating or more favorable for the existence of life on Earth. The second reason could be specie specific, which means that human beings should build a social order that may bring forth the evolutionary strength of the human specie to an even greater degree.

Freedom to compete with other fellow human beings, while behaving as strangers to each other, may induce undesired results: The brutal methods of exploitations may kill and destroy the weaker sections of the population and reduce the strength of survival of the community, where the labour and toil of these people may constitute the backbones of the social-economic development. A fierce competition by intelligent people in defence of individual freedom and success without caring for norms that may safeguard and protect others from misery and unhappiness, will give rise to a society where unity and cooperation among the members of the community will fall apart and expose the society to outside danger. Without loyalty and trust of the majority of the members a social order is bound to perish. When religious views no longer can support the moral backbones of the society, and knowledge of science has opened up the paths of relating oneself to the world in a innovative way, which can link human beings across nations and continents with digital communication, the needs to find moral ideas that may build trust among human beings across the globe have become precarious. The fierce global competitions in supplying consumer products and win greater sizes of the global market as a strategy of survival of a society against its competitors, without sharing a common human value which may build trust among the human beings, is bringing the present global-order into a path of brink.

Without the help of heaven, following the spirit of nature, which inspires trust and cooperation among the kin, the humanity should realize the kinship with each other. The idea of sharing and cooperation need to be extended beyond the closest kin, related by blood, to include wider variations of the genes producing different traits and abilities of the human characters. Instead of letting one gene to win and dominate the others, there must be a cooperative effort in bringing several aspects of the human genes to succeed together. The society must be more holistic in approach and less supportive of one or a few particular trait to dominate and win. Freedom should be enhanced to include the larger sections of the population by increasing the value of knowledge and opening up its access for the majority. Knowledge about the world and secure environment of cooperation and trust will bring those, who possess narrow views and fall prey of weaker abilities, out of the "prison".

One must ensure freedom of creativity, originality and self-fulfilment and search in one`s personal way, without trampling the idea of brotherhood and solidarity with fellow human beings which may bind the people of all nations of the world as members of the same family. In the way compassion and love work in a smaller social-unit, like in a family or among friends, the higher values of life that build trust and bind human beings together in inseparable bonds must be the priorities of the higher-social order.

Instead of viewing human beings as clusters of classes, fighting against each other for dominance and extracting advantages of one`s own class and group, the human beings should be made aware of the higher man, who resides in all. The direction of civilization should be geared towards a fuller emergence of this higher-man through our genes, who is willing to make sacrifice as expression of love for the living world.

Love is the most important power of all that can transform the non-living world into living beings and bring regeneration from death to life. One should learn to see the formation of the biological molecules and DNAs as the acts of love - a cosmic manifestation of a power that animate everything - from living to the nonliving beings. We should learn to retrieve our religiosity through the path of knowledge of science by understanding the great mystery of the cosmos and our position and relations with it. This could be the foundation of moral values which may guide and direct humanity towards building a social-order of higher-man of the future (I have discussed about these values based on cosmic perspective in the book "Vision of An Enlightened World")[1].

---

1   For information visit http://BooksOfExistence.no

MORALITY, BIOLOGY AND COSMOS

In talking about morality the first thing comes into mind is the way it subjects the behavior of the individuals to a common social understanding of what is good and bad, or right and wrong. The concepts of right and wrong have very often a social function: It prohibits the actions (and the thoughts which inspire such actions) which are against the interests of security and survival of the community. The actions which may expose the society to dangers of being invaded by the enemies, or reduce the resources of productions on which the survival of the population depends, are termed wrong and bad actions. On the other hand any ideas, thoughts and actions which can promote the security and improve the conditions of living of the people, are termed right and good. So most moral are selfish moral, which serve the needs and necessities of the social group which attaches values to actions as good and bad to increase its defense against the competitors and the threatening forces of nature and the predators.

Morality gets institutionalized with the development of the society: Some takes the role of the authority, whose tasks are to implement and realize the practice of the morals in the society in an effective way, so that the intention of the moral are preserved. The moral authority in turn takes support of the people who can enforce the values with power, if needed. Rules, regulations, norms are established and institutionalized and protectors of the institutions are chosen. It gives birth to tradition and the way of policing the population against violations of norms and rules imposed by the moral authority.

Every society is a collection of individuals with varied capacity of brain and intelligence. Those, who are less informed and lacks stimulation and belief in one's own capacity, become easy to rule and control in the society, once the basic security may be guaranteed. The more intelligent ones, who are more informed about the world and have wish to explore the world in their personal way, may find the moral imposition critical to their desire for freedom. They often seek ways to increase their personal freedom at the cost of the benefit of the common good of the community. All societies have to deal with this tension between the smarter genes, and the common genes, who are happy to sacrifice freedom once the basic conditions of living and producing are in place. In societies, where the tension is sharper, the morality takes meaning relative to the way the society diversifies into different categories of human beings: An example is the Hindu caste system, which is essentially based on the nature of labour and activities in which the social members are involved. Brahmins, who lived on metaphysical speculations and conducting religious rituals had their own specific set of morals,different from the moral applied for the casteless who were the most insecure economic group living in ignorance and mental darkness. In such a society the definition of moral also became the preservation of these different sets of morals for different groups, instead of bulldozing a single set of rules for all. The moral became the actions that conformed with rules allotted to the caste, to which one belonged. By following caste rules one could gain merit of karma (actions) of this life, which would show its results in the next life.

Clever genes have clever ideas! More clever was the authority in imposing moral in the society, more abstruse and diffused became the foundations of moral. As most people had a curiosity to know who was controlling everything happening around them in nature -for example, driving the cycles of life and death, and were fearful of the natural forces,which threatened life, the idea of the existence of Heaven became the best way to control the society. In many societies the moral was tagged with religious views and ideas. The association of Heaven behind the social rules and norms became an effective tool for the authority to impose the constraints on personal freedom. Fear of Heaven also could be used in mobilizing the mass against the behavior the society did not condone.

In some societies with more material abundance and less insecurity of survival, where individual were more reflective and freedom seeking, metaphysical arguments were necessary to bring free thinker under an umbrella of belief. The moral ideas were substantiated with philosophical reasons and a views about the nature of the world, which people could not reject easily.

Once the economic necessities were no more precarious issues of life, and the fear of invasion from outside seemed remote, the societies developed a more evolved ground for moral, that called for an understanding of the nature of existence of the world and life. One example is the Hindu metaphysics, which became the foundation of moral, which involved the ideas of compassion and universal altruism.

Less intellectual society, referred to faith in Heaven and God as the foundation of moral and reverted to methods of punishment and social sanctions as the ways to bring the nonbelievers into the moral fold.

History of religion has shown us how religions have been abused and manipulated in controlling and depriving human beings of their freedoms to explore the possibilities of life in many societies. Religion has also often been an instrument of the individuals willing to ascend to power and take control of resources of the society to the advantage of a few, and life in misery for the many. In feudal societies the religious leaders and the landowning class have worked hands in hands: The feudal landlords have provided economic resources and man powers to strengthen the religious foundations of the society, whereas the authority holding the keys to moral conduct in the name of heaven have allowed the men in power to trespass laws and rules and remained loyal to the social-order which needed each other for their own interests of keeping power and wealth in their hands.

The basis of this morality, revolving around which group and power interests have triumphed over the rest, has changed with new economic opportunities and changing conditions of society, often taking place under the time of invasion, or intrusion of other beliefs and faiths in the society.

One example is the rise of the scientific knowledge, which has changed the conception of the world and the role human beings may play in organizing their own destiny without appealing to heaven or any other-worldly power. The intelligent innovators and seafarers looking for wealth and opportunities outside the social boundaries confined by feudal-religious values, brought a fundamental change in our understanding of moral values.

The rise of the businessmen and bankers who expanded the economic activities to industrial production and the expansion of the traders to markets in far way countries,which became colonies, brought new aspects to moral that heightened the value of the individual freedom to achieve success. Many of the successful traders and businessmen were not willing to submit their rights and freedom to the traditional moral values of the religious-feudal origin. The arguments on heaven became less and less appealing to the smarter genes. Instead, the rights of the individuals to explore and seek the conditions of life appropriate for oneself, without coercion of state or any central institutions, took a more prominent place in deciding the moral platform of a market oriented individualistic society.

The grievances of the impoverished mass, who were exploited in the traditional oligarchical society, were exploited to arouse people in revolt against the existing social structure in order to replace it with new social values of freedom and rights of the individual human beings.

In this way too, the selfish genes again returned. In the new industrial world, where heaven receded at a distance and the power of the traditional ruling class based on landed properties was reduced, the banker and speculators rose to take the advantage of the new market mechanism based on money, interests and capital accumulation and exploitation of workers. Those who could create more money by taking interests on loans, or making profits by producing and selling products in the market became the new force to decide the moral premises of the society. By paying less for the labour and selling the products at higher value in the market they introduced a mechanism of exploitations of the workers, who had nothing but labor as their assets to sell for making a living. With this development there increased emphasis on the rights and freedom, which could uphold the greed for money and power of the rising class.

The freedom and power of the money making capitalists and their methods of exploitations brought the educated middle class, who was being informed about the knowledge of science and various philosophical and social thoughts from different cultures through the growth of educational systems, to react. The educated middle class, who hang between the workers and the capitalist owners, gave birth to radical groups who mobilized social forces for liberating the exploited workers from the hands of the new economic power elites. It brought socialist revolution, which emphasized on the freedom of the workers and their rights to control the economic production and distribution in the market in a morally viable way. In their view the morality was to curtail the freedom of the capitalists and increase the freedom and benefits for the workers instead.

So what is good and bad, or right and wrong in the society has often been decided by those who have controlled and decided over the economic resources in the society. Economy has been seen as the prime mover of morality. The metaphysical views and philosophical speculations were necessary to give the different moral ideas their legitimacies. With changing economic opportunities these philosophies have also changed. Within this general dynamics of the changing moral in the society, based on economic benefits and security, the poles of tension in the society have remained more or less the same: On one side selfishness that inspires people to grab most for himself/herself at the expense of the misery and pain of others; and on the other side an altruism that motivates people to come to help of those who are suffering in the society. Altruism to do good to others by some are often hijacked by the smarter genes, who see opportunities for their personal gains in the new conditions which has emerged. Selfish genes again and again try to take control of the social goods and benefits. This freedom and greed of a few again and again create new conditions of suffering in the society, which implants discontent and give birth to altruistic ideas and actions. The changes that follow such altruism again give opening to the forces which may take advantage of the changed situations, which may wish to implant selfish motives in the society again.

Thus morality has no permanent ground. What is morally right today may turn out to be morally wrong tomorrow. It exists as a way to reduce suffering of the people, caught in a social condition where one must produce, reproduce and live while enjoying some degree of security. The acts which contribute in increasing security and reducing sufferings of people are often seen as good acts of life.

However, the constantly changing world can not bring a permanent state of security and happiness to people for all times. Every social condition sows the seeds of contradictions in the form of will and desire that inject selfish freedom into the social dynamics. Without this element of individual freedom the will can not adjust to the conditions of changes occurring in the world. The moving world outside oneself generates the contradictions that appear as the force of selfish will trying to take advantage over the weakness of the others in areas where the gene is functionally more adaptive and efficient. Thus new conditions of sufferings appear, which in turn bring forth the power of altruism and social change once again.

So good and evil go hand in hand. Without the presence of one the other has no ground to take place. By accepting this dialectics of good and evil, one should define morality, which prescribes the way one may free oneself from a particular state of bondage and at the same time create new grounds where freedom leads to a new form of bondage. One may say that it is the way through which all existence must pass in order to evolve in the world.

The tension between the opposite that bring good and evil as moral dictum of existence, can be easily illustrated by the conflicts between the Christian morality of sympathy for the weak and the meek and the idea of Nietzsche, which puts the freedom of the brave and the powerful as the highest moral essence of life. Christianity sees a way to accommodate the less successful people in the community as equal and guarantee them happiness and security as a moral path to follow, while the other sees it as a way of following a "herd-morality" which debase the higher-nature of man. For the Nietzschian thinkers the goal to achieve the highest possibilities of life by using will and motivation to fulfill higher nature of man is the path to moral ascendancy. For them the path prescribed by Christianity is a moral dungeon created by love for the poor and the weak.

The history has seen the rise and fall of both views of morality. The contradiction between the way to judge right and wrong has been the major force behind the success and failure of social evolution.

Both views have ideological supports from different philosophical camps: The philosophy that professes unity of all life as originating from the one, and proposes the way to improve one's happiness by doing good to all, leads to altruistic thoughts. This view implants sentiments of compassion and love and inspires human beings to make sacrifices for the others, who may be suffering in life. The other camp squarely puts the blame of suffering on the human beings who lack the will to rise and free themselves from the conditions which may try to imprison and make a slave of them. Nietzsche will call them as lower human beings, who does not make use of the power of the will to ascend and reach the apex of the human mind, that can radiate power and energy to illumine and inspire humanity to see the super human power residing in the mind. For these philosophers the higher man is the one who trudges the paths of suffering in order to attain the highest summit of the mountain in oneself. The higher-man is the bearer of the power of evolution and growth, which the universe has endowed on us.

In the modern time the universal basis of morality has found expressions in the Declarations of Human Rights by the United Nations. One set of rights emphasizes on the rights of the individuals to express their freedom in choosing the systems of governance, political association and ideological groupings and liberty of free speech, individual opinions, choose religious belief and worship. The other set of universal rights involving social, economic and cultural rights stress more on the rights of the groups and people and the common benefits the society may harness from cooperation and responsible enactment of individual freedom. The main tension between the individual and the group as regards what is right and wrong are expressed in a different form through these Declarations.

The successes of the forces that stand behind one set of rights, or the other depend on the economic and political powers which the proponents of individual or peoples' rights may have achieve in the society. The socialists stress on the rights of the people by curtailing the rights of the individual freedom; the capitalists in turn give emphasis on the rights of the individuals and less control by the state or the community.

However, the ideas of sharing and ameliorating suffering of the others have support from both. For the individualists the compassion is often a religiously motivated value. They see it as a way to gain benefits from heaven and increase happiness either in this life or in the next life. The atheist socialists, who believe in dialectical materialism instead of heaven and God, pursues it as solidarity with the exploited ones, in order to accelerate the class struggle that will establish socialism at the end and free the world from the "drug of religion".

Similarly the supporters of individual freedom fall across religious believers and the atheists. The smarter genes always look for opportunities of self-fulfillment and exploration outside what are socially imposed on the majority. They look for ways to evolve in new directions.

Thus both sentiments - sharing and compassion for the suffering people and the desire for freedom that may lead to self-realization without

56

being a prisoner of established morality of the society - are universally operative behind the activities of the human beings in all ages and cultures. Religions and ideologies have paved paths for both the sentiments to shape the world and civilizations. They have acted as vehicles to express the fundamental dialectics of morality in life.

Some philosophical religions, like Hinduism and Buddhism, have accounted for both the elements of morality i.e. altruism and compassion and freedom for the realization of the self, by building views about how the world is created and how things are unified as One, and which responsibility one bears about self-realization. The idea of the unity and immortality of the soul is prevalent in these religious-philosophical views. Altruism and compassion follow as actions benefiting the self by preserving and securing the well-beings of the others, who are parts of the same self. Doing harms to others are seen as inflicting pain on oneself.

In the same religious context one also talks about the acceptance of the reality of the world where people possessing different mental awareness live: Some are stooped in darkness and ignorance unaware of the possibilities of freedom, which one may gain through knowledge and insight, beyond the needs of securing the basic necessities of reproduction and survival. For others, who may have received some knowledge and information about the nature of the world where one may seek newer grounds for self-fulfillment, the desire for freedom expands outside the conditions decided by the environment and social morality. With it individualism grows. When knowledge reaches a higher level, and one gains wisdom about the functioning of the cosmos and our place in it as a part of a cosmic being manifesting through all, the freedom seeks to free all who live in the bandages of ignorance which steal the possibilities of self-realization as a part of the higher-man (note that I do not use the word "higher-man" to mean the same as what Nietzsche did).

In such a mixture of mental capabilities and awareness existing in a society, morality becomes an amalgam of diverse desires to act, that become the source of social conflicts and sufferings for oneself and others. However, it is an inevitable reality of any society as long as long as all, who live in the social arena, have not reached a wisdom that can remove conflicts of freedom from the world. Such conflict free state of existence has been described as the state of Buhdhahood and Nirvana in Buddhism, for example. In reality it means that such a state has no reality in the world, where living creatures have their home.

So, as the Buddhists say, suffering is the essence of life for the human beings, except those few who have learnt to reduce conflicts with the help of inner orientation to reality called wisdom. Suffering is therefore the foundation on the basis of which morality receives its meaning.

How to function in life believing in the idea that all others belong to the same self as oneself and united as a part of the cosmic being in One, and therefore refrain from doing harm to any other being, while at the same time one must live in a reality where conflicts and sufferings are inevitable aspects of existence? This most challenging contradiction put ideas of morality to test. It has been difficult to find a consistent rational argument without submitting to the contradiction. Less philo-sophical religions sees the futility of rational arguments and prescribes religious scriptures as the only way to follow.

More philosophical religions instead try to deal with this question at length and find an intellectual exit from the philosophical tangle which may seem impossible to resolve. Best example is Bhagavat-Gita, the religious-philosophical book of the Hindus, which discusses how to choose the right path when life is full of war, conflicts, and competi-tions among human beings possessing diverse mental awareness about the world and the self.

In trying to resolve the moral problem without abandoning the view of oneness of all and the value of compassion for the suffering world, the Hindu philosophy puts the intentions behind the acts, than the acts committed in reality, as the basis of moral. If the intention behind killing and inflicting suffering to others can free the majority living in the world from greater suffering, then such actions can receive a moral sanction. Moral is also defined from mind`s orientation and views,

58

which prompt such actions. Here the concept of the ego, which arises from the ignorance and delusion, and deprives one of the truth that exist behind the world and the will, and the awareness of the higher nature of the will, which can free a person of ignorance and delusion, become essential in judging any moral meaning of actions. The intentions, which spring from a awareness of the existence of the higher cosmic man in oneself, receive important focus in moral judgement. When delusional ego makes place for the higher-being residing in oneself, intentions are no more seen as bound to the ego and the individual. Instead they originate from a cosmic power, which acts in the world to bring harmony and order in the universe. Thus the wisdom of the universe bear the responsibility of one`s ego-less actions in life`s war and struggle.

In such moral philosophy one is asked to act without claiming that the ego-bound man is the one who is acting: One is only an agent of the higher-will. Remembering that all actions are necessary for fulfilling the will, which springs from God, one is asked to remain detached from the results of the actions one may take. Thus one can change the focus of intentionality from the delusional ego to the cosmic necessity in preserving the order of existence. It professes: Act without believing that your are acting by submitting the ego to the meaning and purpose of the existence of all.

It is a way of self-negating and positing oneself as a part of a higher-being, who is not touched by conducts, which can be called right or wrong. In this thinking too, morality rests in fulfilling the will of God. It is only more complex and abstract in its way of argumentation.

How does science support the moral standpoints which include both altruism and compassion for others, as well as the freedom of the individuals in pursuit of one`s own happiness and development?

Biology, of course, confirms the unity of all living beings - starting from bacteria to the human race. All are made of the same elemental stuff forming amino acids and the nucleic acids. The different arrangement of base pair molecules in the DNA double helix strand make the variations of life forms. The differences of characters, traits and mental capacities can be traced to the genetic code.

Life supports each other and live on each other. We can not create all amino acids ourselves. We need to consume other plants and animals to get the required amino acids for our existence. In the living world, all depend on all in order to maintain the spectrum of living species we observe on Earth. For example, by eradicating the bees, we may eradicate the whole of the animal world, who are dependent on flowers and fruits for survival. The deaths of the bees will bring the method of reproduction by pollination to a halt. Similarly to the insects, all life have definite roles to play in the ecological system on Earth. By harming a small part of it one may eradicate a large number of species. So respect and reverence to all life appear necessities for the existence of life of all.

Inflicting suffering can be interpreted as bringing disharmony in the relations between the living creatures and nature. By disturbing the ecological balance in which life hangs together one can destroy the fine equilibrium which life has established with the physical environment. A body flinches in pain when the holistic functioning of the organs, forming the body, can not create a balanced and harmonic adjustment with the surrounding conditions. Intentionally to inflict such pain on a living creature, biologically seen, can be an immoral act. When actions and motives promote harmony and balance in nature, conducive to thriving of life, one may call them biologically good acts.

It resonates much with the religious-philosophical idealism professed by many cultures. However, the living creatures also feed on each other in order to continue to survive. On the sacrifice of the species of lower intelligence the specie of higher intelligence evolve and thrive. One calls it the evolutionary struggle and fitness. So one may wonder how to define moral in this world of the predators and the preys.

By preying on the weaker ones the evolution eliminates the creatures of lesser intelligence and makes place for the species of higher mental capacity, who can express will and freedom at a higher level of consciousness, which is not constrained by the dictates of the physical world. The preying acts open room for the evolution of species of higher intelligence. In human sphere it inspires the desire for freedom to evolve towards a higher-man.

Life brings to everybody the challenges of making adjustments and compromise of freedom which can reduce conflicts so that an orderly functioning of the society can be sustained. Preying for finding means to live and survive become ethically allowed as long as one does it from the necessity of nature, and not as a project to destroy the rhythm of nature which maintains a fine balance of all living creatures with the physical environments. When taking life becomes nature's way of sustaining order, the questions of morality may need a different approach than the idea of not doing harm to any life in any circumstance.

Biologically one may discuss it as a question of transcendence - a natural path to give birth to life possessing higher intelligence, who can help the living world to transcend beyond the will which is bound to the physical events of the world. This will lead to the arguments of Nietzsche about the higher-man, which may appear repugnant to many. Why benevolence and compassion for the weak have such appeal to moral thinking if it is not the way the nature has ordained the existence of life? Is non-violence and reverence to all life anti-biological and contradictory to nature? Is it a false teaching that one should cast off, as Niezsche has argued?

Many neurobiologist may argue that there are neurons in our brains which can mirror/simulate the experiences of sufferings as neural actions in the brain, though they are not caused by the physical events occurring in reality. They become activated by internal emotions and thoughts. They are purely mental: The psyche causes somatic experiences of suffering in a situation where causes of sufferings are not rooted in the world. One can argue this as the origin of altruism and compassion. It is the memory of the experiences of the specie which we carry in our neuronal reactions determined by the genes. By retrieving the experiences from memory, this could be a way to take guard of the dangers in nature and thus remain alert about the strategy to be used in case of necessity of flight from the undesirable conditions.

If one wishes to stretch this rational arguments to its end one may even call it as a strategy of self-love. As long as the sentiment of compassion does not lead to endangering one`s own life and making a sacrifice for the other, who is suffering, this sort of neuronal mirroring actions in the brain is only a reaction of the stipulated fear of danger that may occur in reality and affect oneself. It is a way to take guard mentally against the occurrence of such a situation. So one can see it as an is-sue of self-interest. The way of feeling aghast while seeing others suffer may have origin in this self-love and self-interest. Experiments have shown that monkeys, chimpanzees also mirror such compassion in the brain when they see other primates are suffering.

However, there exist universal love, which is not confined to this self-love. It inspires man to sacrifice life for the others without being moved by any interest that serves oneself. It is a sacrifice for the benefit of mankind and its progress and evolution towards a higher-man. In Christianity this is expressed in the sacrifice of Jesus Christ. He is de-picted as the one, who has sacrificed his life on the cross in order to take on himself the sufferings of others on himself. It is an act of love, where no self-interest is involved.

How can this sort of love be foundation of moral in a world where dying for one can be the way of living for others? If the evolution is a competition of the living creatures to find a ground of survival at the cost of life of others, what is this love, and how does it bear any mean-ing in the context of the biological world?

It can be difficult to understand this love by using rational arguments and knowledge of science. One can, of course, see it a power to heighten awareness of the mind about the existence of the being, who is above self-love and self-interest. By this argument one again steps into the idea of the divinity, who can not be understood, and whose love could be the foundation of all existence.

Anyway, it is metaphysics and the truthfulness of such an idea can not be proved. Its existence can only be felt by looking into the inner experiences within oneself. It is a power that appears through the emergence of the higher- mind. The more evolved the mind, the more intensely this power manifests in human life. Unless one`s awareness and consciousness has reached a stage of the higher-man, who is able to experience this power, there exists no other way to know that such love exists, and it has a meaning in the context of the living world.

From personal experience one may argue that it is a power that sees the necessity of sacrifice as the way to keep the world existing. Without a sacrifice for the benefit of the others the world may have ceased to evolve and free itself from the bondage of the physical world. The sacrifice can be a way to attain the higher realm of consciousness, which may connect one to the experience of God. Those who claim that they have "seen" God "sees" the world as a realm of love where all beings are manifestation of God radiating the power of love in all. It can not be proved; it can not be known; it can be felt and touched. It can only be attained by attaining the consciousness of great love.

So religion returns again! One sees the end of the arguments, based on the reason and rational thoughts, which must refer to the physical world and its laws so that they can be comprehensible to the logically arguing mind. Love appeals; universal love brings the existence of divinity close to the mind; it consoles, soothes and acts as balm for the suffering soul. Though it can not be understood, known or grasped, it remains as the indicator of the existence of the power that can stir minds, who have attained higher-stage of evolution.

Those, who have no experience of this love, may consider it as a fanciful thought and do not find arguments how some mind may experience God and others can not? Why does the distaste about the existence of God arise in some mind? Can the experience of this great love be manipulated by manipulating the neuronal mechanism of the brain? In such case what is God?

Of course, many more difficult questions can be asked, which can not be resolved with one answer which can be understood and appreciated by everybody in the same way. All understanding are dependent on personal experiences, genetic makeup of the person, and environmental inputs. I believe that the experience of great love can be lost or gained by changing the brain structure, which is the site through which all experiences emerge bearing qualities and awareness of the mind. However, it is only a vehicle through which the power of love manifests in the world. Like an electric bulb it may glow and dim according to the input of power flowing through it. The capacity depends on the genes, environment and the way one may train the mind to evolve further from its present state.

Once again, the question if the above thoughts may represent only fanciful speculations of some brains, wired with the feelings of love, which in reality is illusory, may appear in the minds of the sceptics. How can one assure oneself of a firm ground on which the ideas of morality may be conceived and defended without falling victims of illusion and speculation.

Here comes my understanding of the universe. It is the universe of which all are parts. How we have found our place in this universe builds the fundament of values and meaning of existence of life.

I shall delve on the questions of morality from my understanding of the universe, which is different from the mainstream theory of the creation by a big-bang (A short description of my understanding of the universe is given in my book "Timelessness in Time".)

The values and ethics, based on the new view of the universe, are discussed in another book "Vision of an Enlightened World: A Cosmic Perspective". I shall briefly go through it once again here.

According to this view, the universe has a plan like a cosmic symphony, where from the tinniest to the largest structures all are tuned to play in synchronization to create the orchestra eternally being staged everywhere in all scales in an incredible perfection. Although every note being played is impermanent, everything must die to returns again and again creating infinite variations of forms and existence in time. The musical melody being played through births, evolutions and decays remain eternally the same. In an entangled micro and macro-cosmos every existence has a role to play in sustaining the existence of the whole while maintaining a design of the universe which reappears in similar way from the largest to the smallest structures. Inputs from large to small and feedback from small to large uphold the wonder of existence, which represents a harmony and order beyond comprehension of the human mind. Amidst life and death, through the process of annihilation and creation, going on at the same time, the universe emanates everywhere as an unfathomable wonder. It exists as a being above all beings who conducts every variations of the symphony of the whole.

Here meaning lies in the freedom of realizing the role of the self without being hindered and falling apart from the symphony of the whole, where all participate as parts. Thus there is a meaning in discovering an identity, who is seeking expression of freedom as part of the great love (the all encompassing power that unites all) that animates everything in the universe. For the higher-man it lives outside the joy of hearing the drumbeats of the ego-bound ignorance. Instead he/she attunes the mind fully to the supreme consciousness which animates the creation. Thus the higher-man brings forward the evolution of the brain to a newer stage. With this mindfulness one can connect one's existence beyond the physical state of things in space and time, and forge a link with the cosmic dynamics which is churning a process of consciousness in the brain. The ethical and moral premise of life gets altered with the transcendence of the mind from the brain activities, tied to the world-bound environment and perceptions, to the consciousness empowering all, which is free from the physical bondage of the world.

In a social order, where human beings are free from the basic needs, and liberated from the cultural dogmas and prejudices, and enjoy opportunities of engaging in the pursuit of higher freedom, which may open richer dimensions of life, human beings are able to descry the next realm of freedom representing the higher stage of evolution of the society. This expanded freedom brings transcendence of the human life through the emergence of a higher form of consciousness, which may open the doors to explore beyond the limited understanding of life by using the knowledge and methods available to man. This is a way to move beyond the world of material bondage and enter into a union with all that exist in the cosmos i.e. God. The first step of realizing this freedom is the compassion, and respect and love for all. In realizing one's oneness and connectedness with all beings, who exist as wonders of the universe, the life may move forward to reach an enlightened stage of evolution. It is like moving out of darkness to light that opens the vision of existence, not ascertainable by knowledge and reason alone. This consciousness is the source of the true morality in life.

The above discussion of morality may appear tenuous for many readers to follow. Therefore here I give a simpler summary: Good and evil arises from the existence of will that acts in the world in order to fulfil a goal and serve a purpose, which a person intends to accomplish. The definition of good and evil takes different meaning according to the perspectives from which one makes the ethical judgment. In the lowest sphere, where man behaves as an animal, the will to live and act in order toisit survive, reproduce and safeguard the progeny could be judged as sound ethical acts, though others may perish as results of these pursuits. Seen from a situation, where physical survival against the predators is not any longer any urgent necessity, the will to steal others of their freedom and the means of subsistence, which can create conflict and chaos in the society, can be called an evil act. The goodness may be defined as the aspect of the will which seeks to create order and harmony in a world, where others participate and strive in building a common ground of security of survival for all. The wilful acts aimed to exploit physical or mental weakness and ignorance of others in order to organize and lead a social process, which promotes the advantages of a few over the majority, are contrary to the development of harmony and peace in a society. The will, which sees the power of human organization in bringing forward the higher nature of man, creates the foundation of good in the society. It brings forth order and harmony through co-operation and sharing. Those, who promote the knowledge of the enlightened world, and act with the awareness of the unity of all, and inspire others to march towards realms outside the boundaries of ignorance, and thus draw humanity towards a larger world beyond the sphere of the instincts, could be considered as the bearer of the power of "good".

Read more about good and evil in chapter 5, SOURCES OF VALUES: UNDERSTANDING OF THE UNIVERSE AND OURSELVES in the book "Vision of An Enlightened World".[1]

---

1   For information visit http://BooksOfExistence.no

Part II

A GUIDE TO MORAL

COMPLEXITY AS REGARDS THE QUESTION OF MORAL

The primary purpose of this Guide to Moral is to set a perspective about the questions of morality by taking the help of the knowledge of physical, biological and social sciences.

Moral questions, I have dealt with, relate to the human beings made of biological matter possessing a will with which they interact with the physical environment and seek an arena of freedom for reproduction, survival and growth. The artificial creatures made as robots, who can be programmed to simulate intelligence and decision making process of the human beings at a primitive level fall outside this discussion.

The problem of moral gets more and more complex as we see human life from the perspective of biology and evolution, and know how this biological life is embedded inside a complex entanglement of the micro- and macro cosmos. In every level there are interactions of many in the process of forming and sustaining the existence of any single life. Starting from the radiations coming from the sun, and the movements of air and water churned by the gravitational pull of the cosmic orbs to the inhalation and exhalation of breaths of the living beings are all intricately entangled to form the basis of existence we enjoy.

By destroying one of these intricate pathways, through which life sustains itself, one would destroy the whole balance and jeopardize our existence of life on Earth. Everything has its natural rhythm and propensity by which it seeks to interact with the world. One can call it a natural wisdom, which is too complex for analysis by the human mind. One can view it as the wisdom of the whole i.e. the entire universe and all beings embedded in it. Call it God, or anything else is only one`s own choice of semantic.

In this natural rhythm things appear under the tensions of forces, and disappears in the same way; life comes and goes as natural cycle of life and death; mind emerges and sinks in the stream of animated world; will asserts itself as freedom from the drag of matter and submits itself to the higher will in order that all may exist as one creating the rhythm and harmony which can not be undone. One may call it destiny (if one so wants): In this destiny there exists freedom to move, act, change course following the inner power of the mind in order to return and unite with the force from which mind has sprung.

Seen from individual perspective, the life is churned by tensions of many forces moving in different directions at the same time, trying to come in a fine balance with the whole in order to find a natural place for the individual life concerned. This tension is often described as the source of suffering of life.

It is always there, and will be there as long things exist in the universe. Will is a sort of foam sprinkling out of this churning of the world: The energy and power driving the universe appears as will to establish control and power over the material movements which creates the churning. It acts as its own master bringing back order in any chaos that may ensue.

Life has appeared from this churning through many phases, which we call evolution. The will has manifested in many levels of awareness about the world: One may call them the levels of consciousness. From primitive life with a few neuronal cells to the human beings with billions of neurons, the mind has evolved as activities of the brain. The more evolved the brain more power it possesses to control the conditions that appear as result of churning of the material world. It appears as power to assert freedom of the mind over matter. The existence thus appears as two arena: One is the world controlling the contents in which the mind manifests; and the other is the mind which keeps watch over the world and guides it to follow the rhythm and harmony of the universe. The existence is two-fold: Matter and mind. However, neither precedes the other; they are always in unison and eternally existing as one. In that sense the universe is suffused with mind, which I call the cosmic mind. One may call this as God.

Coming down from the cosmos, when moral issues relate to activities of the human beings in the social context, it becomes highly complex and nearly intractable to follow by intellectual reflections.

Most societies include human beings of different mental capacities and awareness: Some mind are still groping in the darkness of the primary instincts, like reproduction and survival. Some have achieved power to establish new relations with reality and environment by using knowledge and innovative means. They can expand personal realms of freedom and gain control over others by using information and knowledge. Some may have achieved a deeper understanding of the unity of all and the meaning of freedom outside the realm of personal greed and desire. They are the bearers of the power of compassion and love, which inspire one to serve the society for the good of all. These higher men use their freedom in liberating those who are not free and living in darkness of ignorance. However, no human being bears in himself/ herself only one type of consciousness or awareness. In all human beings all levels are mixed in different weights. The awareness, which dominates one`s consciousness, defines the nature of the person.

Besides this stratification of human beings according to their mental abilities and grades of awareness of freedom in acting and behaving in the society, moral involves relations of individual to many at different levels of social construction. There are relations which involve individual to individual; there are relations where individual interacts with others as a part of a group; some relations are related to the institutions through which one expresses one`s moral attitude and affiliation; and some could be motivated by the identity of belonging to a nation or a race, or an organization that cuts across boundaries of several nations.

Moreover, at each level of this relationship there are several categories of issues one needs to address: some relates to the basic needs of reproduction and survival; some relates to the freedom of exploring the world and experiencing other dimensions of the mind outside the reproductive and survival needs. It also includes the human desire to know about the working of things and taking control of the events happening in the physical world around, and one`s position in the universe and relation to any higher power.

Most fundamental is the need for reproduction and survival in a world where people need to compete with others for the desired goods and opportunities of freedom. Every society works under an economic framework which provides the opportunities and arena to compete. The interactions of human beings in this economic arena demand some rules of the market, and conception of values of one thing compared to the other. Here moral has its character depending on which level human consciousness controls the moral ground, and who controls freedom of the majority in the society. In a capitalist social system it is different from the socialist values, for example.

Besides markets, goods and services needed for economic functioning of a society, desire to know about the world and others and share one`s emotional feelings with others through different forms of communications, like writing, painting, dance and music etc. are expressions of intelligence and evolution of the mind. They may spin around imagination and belief and psychological need to vent out feelings of sufferings and joy encountered in the world. These relations form the cultural interactions in the society. The meaning of moral takes a different hue when one deals with these emotional aspects. It can not governed by the similar values which control the behavior of people in the economic market.

Moral takes again a new turn, when it comes to sharing knowledge and information, which increases one`s economic security and gives advantage to protect and expands one`s territories of freedom. This is particularly the case in matters related to knowledge which concerns military tactics and technology, and the economic resource utilization with innovative means. Revealing these secrets to the others may be considered amoral for those who enjoy fruits of knowledge and information by depriving others of the knowledge; it is, in turn, seen amoral to the others against whom the secrecy is kept. It is amoral because by keeping some knowledge and information as secret, which should be available to all of mankind, a smaller group tries to monopolize power over the rest. Knowledge of science and technology and their use becomes a matter of ethical contention.

Then comes the activities related to the spiritual sphere, where belief, faith, personal prejudices and experiences do not match with the world felt and known by the use of the perceptions, knowledge and reason. It brings an understanding of spiritual moral which may contradict morals practiced in other spheres of activities.

So moral has multi-dimensional components, which may appear as contradictions once activities in one area are judged with activities in another arena. The same man who is pious and seen as morally elevated in the spiritual matter can behave in a morally fallen way in many other fronts of human interactions. Moreover, through the interests and practices of groups, institutions, and nations one define what is moral or immoral for one, which may contradict others`point of views. Moral is thus tangled in such a complex web of individual, group, national and institutional pathways that to define a universal moral for all in the same way seems impossible.

It becomes a doll-drum of philosophy, which can never be resolved by an intellectual debate. Every life is tangled in this mess, where different currents of interests and forces try to shape the social development to gain advantage. The forces which take upper hand becomes the moral progenitors of the group for that time. With history and time, with rise and fall of groups and interests, with ascend and descend of institutions and civilizations the moral premises have constantly moved, as if some invisible hands have been weaving the moral fabrics of the society in new patterns and renewed stable structures all the time.

Things appear good and bad from the perspective of history and time and where one is embedded in the complex entanglement of forces and one`s position in the social structures that constantly move. Moreover the level of consciousness, one possesses, also defines the ground of moral for the person concerned. Intentionality of actions, than the actions in-themselves become less relevant to moral judgement. Intentionality, in turn, involves knowledge, information and insight about the nature of the world and will of which one is a part. Ones, who are more informed and knowledgable and possess a greater insight about the working of the society, becomes more responsible for their acts, than those who are acting and doing as ignorant creatures deprived of the light of knowledge.

Moral can be seen as codes which hold things in place, and weave the small social units into a bigger unit, which can then coalesce into an even bigger unit, and so on... ending in the formation of the global arena. The codes form from the physical state of things, and the social forces competing with each other, and the way people possessing different capacities and awareness of the mind realize their freedom in the world. Moral is a signature of the social evolution through which a society has passed, or is passing.

"Right or wrong" can be another way of stating the conditions that arise due to the conflicts and tensions inherent in any social dynamics (feels as wrong) and the feelings that rise when these tensions and conflicts are reduced by using the higher power of the mind (feels as right). The conflicts are conditioned and produced by the local circumstances, or circumstances specific to the social unit, to which one belongs. Outside this boundary it does not have the same meaning of right or wrong.

So does there really exist no foundation of moral in heaven as religious people have taught, or in reason as professed by the philosophers (for example Kant)?

To answer this question, first one has to change the concept of heaven and see the limitations of reason. If it is assumed that there exits an absolute reason, which is above all interactions and conditions that define our behavior in the world, and transcend all what can be experienced in the practical level, where all must engage with others in conflicts or cooperations in order to achieve personal freedom as well as gain security of existence of all, such pure reason is a sort of dictum which implies the existence of heaven that remains outside the world. If we assert that heaven is within the world and the will, which embrace us in our activities of daily life, then such pure reason has to be abandoned in favour of the existing nature of things.

I shall like to define heaven as the universe itself and God as the power that churns all events in the universe. Through this churning the mind and consciousness can exist, while the cosmic consciousness puts order and perfection in the creation process. God is not a being, who exists outside the realm of the world; nor it is one with the physical world. God is both emanant and existent: The world and mind emanates from God, and God exists within the emanant world. Without God world and will have no existence, and similarly without world and will God has no existence. No one precedes before the other. One`s existence is not causally linked with the other`s, like events of the physical world. Heaven and God is everywhere - even in the grain of sand, or in the atoms and the molecules floating in the cosmos.

When the consciousness evolves at a higher level, like in the creatures on Earth who possess evolved brains, the will becomes revealed in the world as an agent affecting and organizing the creation. The higher the evolution of the brain greater is its ability to reveal the nature of the cosmic consciousness which organizes the universe in its unfathomable complexity. The evolution of man towards the stage where it can reveal more the nature of God through himself/herself is the stage of the higher-man i.e. Man-God (a man in whom the mind of God is revealed in the world).

Thus heaven is one with the world, and God is within us. So the foundation of moral is within us embedded in the world of our activities.

Through us heaven is revealed.

Hell is another way of defining heaven as a falling awareness of the greater nature of the mind which we all share as part of God. When activities lead human mind backward in evolution of specie when it was still constrained by the laws of physical world, and will was covered by ignorance about the nature of things, one sees the regression of life towards a darker realm. More one sinks deeper into the darkness of the primitive world, more hellish the world appears to those who has progressed towards light.

So what should be the moral? What is the right way to act and live?

First, everybody has a different starting point in the journey towards the higher-man, determined by physical environment, gene, history, social conditions, economic opportunities, cultural climate and the opportunities of freedom and cooperation allowed by the people ruling and controlling the resources and institutions.

However, wherever one is, to take a step forward can be a morally advancing act. Every action that brings man towards the realization of the higher-man in himself/herself can be called an ethical action. It includes actions that bring one to a higher path, as well as compassion for the others that inspires one to bring those, who are in darkness, towards light. It is a march forward from darkness to light and a desire to help others to get out of the darkness and see light.

The morals should spring from the realization of the nature of the universe, and the insight into the world and will where God is emanent and existent as the physical world and all which exist as part of the cosmic consciousness. Morality is like a torch that can guide man to see paths through the darkness of the mind, and thus help us to come nearer to the great mind which beckons us all.

So the primary foundation of moral is to gain insight into the higher-nature of oneself and the way one`s will functions in the context of the society, culture, economy etc. and try to use one`s freedom to take a step forward, instead of regressing backward in evolution.

While taking these steps one should communicate to the fellow human beings about the way the others may also act to get out of the darkness of the mind. Bearing the power of love, which seeks to relieve others from suffering, help others to move away from darkness and gain insight into the nature of the higher-man in oneself. Seeking one's own freedom in order to liberate the fellow human beings as brothers and sisters belonging to the same family, should be the universal foundation of moral in all societies and cultures though they may enjoy different stages of economic development.

It is an individual way of progressing together. For this journey together to be successful one needs a moral attitude of the group as a whole which gives freedom and responsibility to the individual to forge a bond with others that may secure the success of the journey together towards heaven and God.

One may wonder who will implant the insight and the vision of the journey towards light to those unfortunate ones who have never seen anything but darkness?

Where the moral actions involve groups and societies it becomes a task for the society to engage the more enlightened ones in the society to lead this work by forming institutional structures that aim at giving insight and knowledge to all without discrimination. This can be the first steps to make the journey out of darkness to light.

How such a morally based ideas, which I have shortly explained here, may function in practice and replace the social-order, which exists today in the world, is described in the book "Enlightened Democracy With Cosmic perspective: A Vision of a New World".

Before finishing this chapter I would like to mention that the discourse I have presented so far is based on intellectual reflection and fully controlled by the mind, which I perceive as me. However, it is very clear to me that the intellect has a limited power to penetrate deeper into the mystery of God and resolve the questions of moral, which may relate to such godly existence.

In the end I would like to add the book "Gita of the Will and the World", which "I" wrote 17 years ago in Seoul. In this book "I" was not the one who was the writer; My intellect had no role in the process. Instead "I" was trapped in a surreal world by another existence who delivered the messages.

Was it God? Or was I affected by a brain disorder?

VALUES BASED IN A REALM BEYOND REASON

GITA OF THE WILL AND THE WORLD

Foreword

The "Gita of the Will and the World" had appeared as automatic writing in the form of streams of words flowing uninterrupted by the intellectual and rational power of the mind, as if, some invisible being was the real author of the book. The pages after pages had flown without hiding to conscious introspection of the content being written. In this unconscious process, I felt as a medium through which a weird world was speaking.

When this happened I believed it to be a revelation and saw my role a receiver of messages from God. Although the messages were addressed to a man who was me, I realized that I was only a part of a greater body, to whom God was speaking. This greater Man, to whom all human beings belong, existed in two different states: In one he was "children of women and men" and in the other he was Son of God – one bound to the body of flesh and blood and whose will is conditioned by the world existing in form, while the other issued from a Divine realm existing beyond the sphere where will was moving in a fate-bound material world.

It became very confusing for me to understand who was the Man to whom God was speaking and how to grasp the enigmatic existence which was divided between the "children of women and men" on one side and someone issuing from God on the other side. Anyway, I realized that there might exist two totally different states to which I, as a part of mankind, belonged: One belonging to Man, and the other to God.

Although God was addressing to Man, he was sometimes speaking as Son of God, and often referring to his existence as Man-God who intervenes in the world, which is bound to matter and form. It was very difficult to understand distinctions between God, existing beyond the matter-bound world and the soul-bound will, and Man-God and Son of God intervening in the world where will resides. Finally I concluded that this cannot be understood using logical and rational thinking. Since then these concepts had remained highly messed up in my mind and I was unable to confirm, or deny the existence of God. I could not be sure if God had any reality, or the "revelation" was only a weird mental phenomenon generated by the brain, which was beyond my capacity to understand.

I present this material for those who are interested in the questions of God and the psychologist and neurologists who would like to understand such weird phenomena generated by the brain.

About entering in the world-and-the will

Follow the will- and- the world as I enter this place and work for the liberation of mankind in blood and flesh. Follow the man you see wearing a human face. Move with Him to Man-God, who is the Savior of the world moving with the world and the will. Follow Man-God as My Son, and make yourself the world-and will's movement. Entering a body and a soul I have entered in the world-and-the will in order to make you move in Man-God's enlightened way. Follow your worldly Savior and make your will one with Him. Follow your worldly Savior, who is not a man, but one with God. Your worldly existence is moving with Him and your existence can not be understood without Him explaining the meaning of the world-and-the will as you hear from Me. Enter the world-and-the will as matter-bound existence and seek in the matter-bound world the worldly meaning of the existence of My Son. Entering the world-and-the will I have entered Myself as Man-God, who is moving with the world-and-the will as Savior of Man.

Keep yourself working for the Man, who is not a man of a particular worldly form. He is the world-and-the will's Savior, who does not move with any worldly desire to make Him different from the formless Self. Knowing yourself as My Son's movement through the world-and-the will come to Man-God, and seek in Him your salvation as Father to His Son. He is working with you, and by working with Him make God move in the world- and- the will as I have made My Son moving with you. Enter the movement, that I have set at work, in order to make man move to Man-God.

Enter Man-God as a matter-bound man and a spirit-bound existence that cannot be made understood by any worldly experience other than your own experience, feelings and thoughts. Your worldly experiences are bound to matter, that make things work as movement of the world of matter contradicting the exotic existence, which cannot be formed with matter. Knowing what you are, move with Man-God, who is moving with you as My Son. Entering the arena of the world-and-the will move as I instruct, and make yourself a movement of Man-God.

Your world is not what you believe it is. Your existence is not what you believe existing as matter and mind. The world of matter is a world of the working force, which creates your body; the world of will is a world of the matter-bound movement of the Spirit, that sees itself in the world as the mind. Your world and will is matter-spirit-bound movement of Man-God, who is moving, working, and seeing Himself in the world as My Son.

Knowing what I have said move and make yourself a vehicle of Man-God, who is the Savior of the world. Knowing what your Father has said, work and make yourself moving in the world as a knower of the Words that have come from God. Hearing these Words move and work following the Mountain-Hermit, who is following His Divine Self.

Birth: Divine and Human

Enter the world-and-the will and know it as My birth place where I have sent My Son. Your world is not matter-bound existence where the will is matter-mind bound. Hear from your worldly Savior about the path of Salvation. Your world is moving while My Son is moving with you. Your world is making a transition from the world-and-the will to Me. Move to Me with Him. How do you know that I am the world-and-the will as My Son dwelling in you, and not the-world and- the will as Man-God appearing as My Son? Know Me through the movement of My Son and His worldly existence as a man of flesh and blood. Know Him as yourself and knowing yourself as Him, seek in Him the world-and-will's salvation. Your world is matter-and will-bound but what is making the will-and-the world is not matter-will bound. Knowing what I have said seek liberation and work as spoken by My Son. Knowing Me as a man, who has taken birth among you as a matter-will-bound existence of a worldly man, work for the matter-bound world's salvation. Knowing Me as your worldly Savior enter the world-and-the will and move.

Know Me as a man of blood and flesh, who has moved to the world-and-the will as a miracle of God. Entering the world I have become Man-God. Man-God is a movement of life and death through a destiny-bound existence, where I am an exotic power that cannot be understood by any one. When I appear in the world-and-the will I have a matter-will-bound existence as well as an existence that cannot be grasped by the matter-will-bound mind. Know Man-God as the exotic existence by which God appears as Soul of a man who is not a man but

God. Know Me as Him, who can exist in both matter-will-bound and not-matter-will-bound states. Know Me as the One who has no birth as God, but who has taken birth as a Man in flesh and blood. Entering the world I have become Man, who is My Son. Know Him as the movement of God. He moves in the world in order to make man move towards Me. The birth of the man, who possesses a darkened body of a human being and the Light of God, is a miracle, which you should not try to understand. Know Him as your friend, teacher and a guide and work as a friend, a teacher and a guide of man whose mind is still darkened by the matter-will-mind.

Know Me as man who has come to life as a Man, who is God. The Man is physically identical to the man you see, and is also the eternal One, who is fate-bound, and exists beyond the realm of time. The man who has a name and a physical identity, which is darkened by the matter-will-mind, is a worldly man like all human beings. The birth of this man has actualized the movement of the Man who has no name and identity. He is working for God. Knowing Me as the man with an identity like you, and at the same time someone who is not a man of any identity work for Me. Know that Father has sent formless Man-God to the world to actualize the existence of His Son. God is born and unborn as Me, who is born of human parents, as well as God and Man-God. Your worldly Savior is Him. Entering the world I am born as Man-God. The world-and -the will is a part of Me. Therefore know Me as born and unborn. Know Father as His Son. Know the formless in form. Know My existence as the world-and-the will, and no-world and no-will. Entering the world I have assumed the roles of a poet, a painter, a philosopher and a man of knowledge and science but really I am no one.

Hear from Me the world-the-will's formless movements in forms, and darkened body's movement from form to formless Man-God. Knowing Him as Me attain the formless existence that has moved among you in a form. God has worked His miracle through Him. Thus know that I exist, and you exist in Me.

Hear: The world's mountains are moving, the climate is changing, the forces in nature are warring against each other, and the bodies are being darkened by the will as a great darkness is overpowering the world. Home and world are moving to the mountains. Man and woman are going to the mountains with Me.

Journey

Entering the world-and-the will, being darkened by the body of a man, and carrying the mind of Man-God, I am making a journey through life. How do I exit out of and enter into the sphere, where the world-and-the will exist, as the power to move the world-and-the will in the destined way, is not available to the knowledge of any man. You must move as I have expressed the world as destiny-bound. Your world does not appear as you may will it to appear. His Will is the will of the destiny-bound world. By willing to move He has destined your movement in the matter-bound path. How do you understand this destiny without being a part of Him? How can man seek Him without being a part of Him? How do you make yourself a part of the world-and-the will without being a part of Him? Born and unborn! Know that I am Him.

How do I understand man and move without being a part of you? How do I make myself moving in the world-and-the will without being made of the world and the will? How do I move without moving into the matter-bound world? Born and unborn! Know that I am moving as Him.

How do you come and go as death and life? How do you assume form as part of life and disappear from the world as death-bound life? How do you know yourself as man and woman in journey through life? Know that coming and going into the world-and ¬the will is world's

94

movement towards Him. Born and unborn! Know that I am with you as part of Him.

Hear from Him: Father has sent His Son to the world-and-the will to make you a part of Him. Powerful movement of Man-God is making the mountains move, causing seas and water of the world to bring torrents and storms. Wanderers! Move with your Savior before the destruction comes.

Journeyman! Work for the movement that I have set in motion, and that will bring to the world a renewal. Know Me as a wanderer who has set His boat in the ocean of the world-and-the will, and is making a journey Home. Know Me as the movement of the wandering Spirit of Man-God, who has come to make you move towards the mountain Home where I have My Heavenly abode. Know Me as Man-God, who makes you work for the world-and-the will, and sets your journey in a destiny-bound path. Know Me as the world-and-the will and no-world and no-will, and make your will and the world a part of Me. Your will and My Will are not in tune when you work for man and not for God. Know your will as matter-bound reflection of the Spirit that sees Itself in the world as images on the river. When I move as you your image creates the world, and the women and men are seen as manifestation of the world in the will, and the will in the world. Your will is moving as the world that cannot be separated from the will that is matter-bound. Your will is moving as a movement of the worldly destiny of man and woman, who come and go with the coming and going of the world. Know the world-and-the will as the work of Man-God, who is moving the world of matter and the sphere of the Spirit as souls of individual women and men.

Know Me as the work of God, who moves the matter and the will as mountains and seas, and the women and men, who are working in the world-and-the will. Know Me as the mountains and seas and the will of all and make yourself journey-bound. Know what is unknown through Me. Know what is working as mountains and seas and not working as mountains and seas. Born and unborn! Know Me as Him.

God has sent Me to guide you in your journey from your worldly home to the Divine sphere. Knowing the meaning of My existence as a poet, who has shown you the worldly form of Man-God, know the world-and-the will as My manifestation in the temporal river. Make the journey as I have made, take the enlightened way, and seek in the world-and-the will your salvation in Man-God. Journeyman! Will not the world, will not the movement that obstructs My Will to come to God. Know My journey as the journey of the will to Man-God and from Man-God to Man and God.

Knowing that the mountains are moving seek through My journey your salvation as parts of Man-God. Know your world as nothing but the will of a worldly man, who is fate-bound. Your world is the world of the working women and men. Know these working women and men through the matter-bound temporal existence of My Son, who is working for Me. Know Him as the journeyman, who is moving in the world-and-the will as the Mountain-Hermit towards Heavenly Home.

Know that I am. Know that I am not. Know Me as Him. Know the world-and-the will as Man and God's fate-bound movement as the Mountain-Hermit. Knowing what I have said work for Man-God. Born and unborn I am the world and the will, and no-world and no-will. Knowing this, seek salvation in Son of God. Journeyman! World is making a transition through the movement of Son of God towards a time when wars and conflicts will destroy that are, as the world-and-the will's destiny, moving towards God. Knowing what you have heard come to sacrifice your life on the altar of God.

Sacrifice

Know what would bring the destruction as I move in the world-and-the will. Know Me as the harbinger of the force that will change the world from the matter-bound existence to the spiritual one. How do you make this transition in the world-and-the will when all should remain in the world and the will? How do you change the matter-bound human existence to the matter-spirit-bound? How do you make all things moving as matter-spirit in the world and the will as Me? Born and unborn I am moving and changing the matter-bound world as willed by Me.

Knowing that I am Man, and Man-God know the meaning of existence of all. Fear not when you hear about the destruction that will arrive. Know the meaning of the destruction that acts in order to make the world-and-the will matter-spirit-bound, and move as sacrifice in the altar where the world will receive its rebirth. Fear not when I come and set the world in turmoil. See Me as the Savior, who sets the world and the will in the path of God. Knowing the world-and-the will as the matter-bound arena of the matter-spirit-soul, where I exist as Man-God, exit the matter-spirit-soul, and create your world and will as I have destined. Fear not what will come. Work for the world's salvation by sacrificing your life. Knowing Me as the coming of God and the movement of the Divine in the world seek in the world your salvation in the existence of My Son. Fear not what works for God. Entering in the world-and-the will I have set the world's salvation in My Son. Fear not what must happen in order that Man-God's existence can be meaningful. Fear not what must intervene in the world-and-the will so that the world can exist as I have desired it to exist. Fear not the world's Savior who is your Father and Son of God. Know that I am attending the sacrifice as your Savior. Make yourself dear to God by moving with World's Soul who will destroy.

God has come and by His coming your existence has received new meaning than what your world-and-the will has been. Knowing what the world is, and what the world is for Man-God, Father has sent His Son. Fear not what He brings, and what path He describes as your path. Fear not the Heavenly Father, and His incarnation. He has sacrificed His Divine existence for the sake of Man. Fear Me not as the One who destroys; fear Me not as the Exotic power that comes as the fate of all. God has moved for the Salvation of Man. Fear not what assumes the world-and-the will. Entering the world I have assumed the world-and-the will, and by the world-and-the will I am working to darken the existence as movement of Will to God. God has worked, and working through the worldly Savior He has come to the world as the fate which will bring destruction. Fear not who is working as world's Savior, and who sacrifices Himself for the Salvation of Man. Fear not what works as God's Love, and the death that He bears for you. God has sacrificed His Son for the salvation of Man. Entering the world I am Him. Enter Me in the sacrifice and be one with Man-God.

Trial and crucifixion

Hear: I am born and unborn; I am external and internal; I am sea and mountain and woman and man; I am fate and fear of all. How do you arrive at Me without being sacrificed to the world-and-the will as My Son? How do you make yourself attain the height of Man-God without being sent to destruction? Exit the world-and-the will and move as I have made My Son move with you. Exit the movement of the destiny bound existence and seek in Man-God your destiny. Know yourself as a fate-bound existence of the worldly incarnation. Born and unborn I am Him.

Exotic power of Man-God is exercising the force to move you to the mountain where I have My Heavenly Home. Human existence is working as anarchy of will that must be destroyed before I am able to seek man's fate-bound existence as Man-God's Soul and form. Woman and man! Your will is working against My Will, and therefore Soul of Man-God is attending your sacrifice for the world-and-the will's Salvation. Will and World must come to Me and death must follow the movement that has made Man-God assume worldly form. He is attracted by will and world as I am making the mountains move, and the seas to bulge. God has made worldly fate-bound existence of the worldly Savior as your path. Entering Me He is Me. He is also not-Me. Exotic existence of Him cannot be known by man. Entering His existence I am one with the world and not-world. His exotic existence is working as My movement as your Savior, who is born and unborn. I have been, and I will be as the World of God.

Knowing what you hear work and act in the way My Son has worked and acted as a worldly man, who is a poet, a painter, a philosopher, and a man of knowledge of science. Trial of the man, who is fate-bound, will come with your trial on the altar of God. Know what your Father has destined: Born and unborn I am the One, who forms the world as destined. How do I know what awaits man far from tomorrow, and the days ahead? Know what is in time and space, and what are making things work in the matter-bound state. Hearing that the mountains are death-bound move as Man-God's sacrifice, and make yourself death-bound. Know what must come, and knowing God's formless movement as Man-God work and act, and make yourself moving to the altar where Son of God is the symbol of sacrifice for the Salvation of man and woman in flesh and blood.

Know what makes Me suffer although there is no suffering in Me. Know what is suffering as the movement of flesh and blood's existence in the will-bound world that cannot know what is not world- and will-bound. Knowing what is unknown work and act and face the trial as woman and man, who are destiny-bound. Crucifixion of Man-God is the symbol of My exotic existence in the world, that has come as a result of the World's Savior appearing as Me. Crucifixion is a peace, and the darkened body's Salvation from the movement of the will that is fate-bound. Crucifixion is the work of God, and world's movement to be released from the matter-bound existence and lift it to the realm of Man-God.

Know what I am, and I am not. Seek in Me your soul's movement to-wards Man-God. Know how the man, who speaks, is darkened and not-darkened by a body of flesh and blood, and seek in Him your fate that is death-bound.

Know Me as God. Know how I bear my physical identity and a name as a man and also exist as Father, who is God. Father has sent Me to the world as your Savior. Crucified on the Cross, I have existed in time that is death-bound. Crucified are the mountains and the seas; crucified are the men and women; crucified is the world-and-the will as Me. Born and unborn! By the world and the will I am crucified to the matter-bound seas and mountains and flesh and blood. Born and unborn! I am your Father. As Son and Father I am God and no-God. Your death is the fate of My Son. Enter Me and seek in Me the adobe of God. Enter sacrifice. Born and Unborn! I am Him. Enter Me and be a part of the sacrifice.

Resurrection

God has sent Son of God as the resurrection of the world-and-the will's Savior for the Salvation of the world. He has assumed a fate-bound movement in form and bears in Man-God the Soul of All. Resurrection of Son of God as an exotic poet is a fate-bound movement, and a formless working of Man-God. He is World, and World is Him as I have sent Him to the world. He has assumed a darkened form. By darkening Himself He has assumed the fate of the world and brought the formless world in form. He has assumed form as body and Soul and has come to you as the Savior who is working for Me. God has worked for His resurrection as God-Man. His coming will bring upon the world destruction. Keep faith in Him. Fail not the words I have spoken before you. God is darkening the world. Enter in Him. Offer yourself as a sacrifice to the altar of God.

Born and unborn! The words of God are Me. Enter the words as Heavenly Father has made them enter the world as words spoken by Me. Enter My existence through the words that you hear, and make yourself the movement of the words that will bring you to Me through these words. Know what these Words mean as the Words of Father spoken through His Son. He is Man-God, who has assumed man's form, and carrying God's formless movement of Words spoken by Me. Enter Words as Man-God's Words emanating from a formless world that makes the words moving in the worldly mind. God's Words are not spoken by any man but a Man, who is God. Have faith in what you hear. Fail not Father and His Son. Fail not Man and God. Fail not to enter the world-and-the will as I have expressed in Words spoken by Him.

God is moving and moving with God make yourself the formless world's movement in form, and seek in Me the Words that you seek in Man-God. Born and unborn I am the darkened world's formless matter-bound existence, which cannot be known by any means other than the Words that you hear. Know God and the words spoken through Me as the Words of God and seek in the matter-bound existence of the man, who speaks, the words that you seek to hear from Man-God.

About God and Man-God

Assume Me not to be a matter-bound physical state and the darkened body that I have assumed. I am not knowable to any man. The Words of Man-God are the only way to know Me. Know God as Father, and knowing Father bear in you the existence that I have assumed. Ear and mouth, that hears and asks, are not what you should use to ask and hear about Me. Your asking to know Me is Man-God's Home-bound movement to the spiritual mountain where questions are answered by Me. How do you ask? How do you listen? How do you attain the power to listen the Words spoken by Me? Have faith in Me and Father. Formless Man-God has darkened His existence in form to make your existence moving with Him. With darkened words and the darkness of the world He has made His Soul darkness-bound. He is a man of Divine birth, and seek in Him the mystery that I have revealed through My Son. How do I exist as a man of human birth, as well as someone who is beyond death and birth? How do I make Myself words of man when no Words from Me are fate-bound? How do I make my existence appear in the world- and-the will when I am beyond world and will? How do I bear a formless existence when I stand in front of you in form? How do I create God's image and man's fate as My Son? How am I nothing but the Words of God but still existing, as you see Me and hear from a fate-bound existence, that I have assumed? How do the Words form and the fate-bound human existence receives the Words, that I speak? Man cannot know this mystery without the existence of My Son who has darkened His existence as a human being and assumed the soul of a man. How do you know what is not knowable? How do you get yourself near to what is not attainable by the down-fallen existence of man in flesh and blood? Have faith in what you hear, and seek what I have sought in making the mountains and seas change the course of the world while the Words are spoken by Me. Know Me as the One who enters and exits the fate-bound existence without being bound to the world-and-the will.

Know God through the Words I have spoken, and seek in the Words spoken by My Son the meaning of the human existence. Faith or no-faith, seek in what you hear the Words of your Savior, who has come to make you move with Him. God has become Man. Man's Salvation exists in Man-God, who has become a Man and Me. Born and unborn I am Him.

Know My Godly existence and seek in My Words the fate-bound movement as man and woman possessing darkened Soul. Though you encounter My Son in a physical state as an existence, darkened like your existence, know Him as your Savior, who brings to you the knowledge of the world that cannot be known. Have faith in Man-God and the Soul of Words that I have assumed. God has moved and make your will moving with Him as My Son is moving in the world. Knowing what you hear from the exotic existence, follow Him and seek in His Words Salvation in Me. God is and is-not. God is working and working-not. Enter what I am and I am-not.

Destiny

Born and unborn the world is Words of Me, and the will is My manifestation as words of those who are born. Know what are the words of the one who is born, and the Words that come from the One, who is unborn. Knowing My existence as Words of the world and the karma-bound existence, that has come to life, work and seek in Words of Man-God the existence of the World's Savior who works as Me. God has darkened the words as spoken, and through these Words I speak as Man-God.

Born and unborn - born as words and unborn as the body of the words that carry the words to the world, born as matter and unborn as matter-spirit-bound will that has no movement in the world of matter as matter - I work and exist as Words moving in the world-and-the will as a Man, who is My Son. God has matter-bound existence only when He Wills to appear as words of worldly man, who speaks like woman and man. Through My incarnation as a man, I am the source of Words to the world. Through this incarnation the Words exit the realm of the Divine. The words spoken by the worldly man, as brought about by a physical existence, are not the Words spoken by Man-God but the man, who is born. Both as Me and Him I am born and unborn as Words of Man-God. God has spoken through Him, and through Him you are receiving the messages from your worldly Savior who has moved as words appearing in flesh and blood. Hearing the Words of the World's

Savior move along the destiny-bound path that I have assumed in My Son. Know what I am as a man of flesh and blood, and what this physical incarnation is not. Know what comes and goes in the physical form and what never appears in the world in a physical form.

Born and unborn! I am darkened words of the physical existence in which I am existing as a poet, a painter and a philosopher-scientist. Coming in the world I am working as a destiny-bound human being. Knowing My movement in the destiny-bound world as the destiny of the world's Savior work and move as man and woman who are darkened by form like my own existence in flesh and blood. He is working for man and woman, who are born, as well as for the woman and man, who are unborn. Know Him, who has come into existence as a man to reveal the Words of Man-God.

Born and unborn with Him your soul is mountain-bound. Son of God is the WORLD and you are parts of Man-God in the exotic existence of the Words of God. Destiny of all is moving with Him. Knowing the World's Savior, as the moving words of the destiny-bound world, move and work as I have destined.

Matter-spirit-bound words

Bear in mind that the words, that I speak, are the words not spoken by Me but spoken by My Son. God and man cannot communicate without God's Son communicating as God to man. Have faith in God-Man, who is matter-bound man and spirit-bound world and will that springs from no-matter and no-will. Know the spirit-bound existence of the world-and-the will and seek in God-Man Salvation through the Words of My Son. Knowing Me as the source of the Words, and knowing the Words, as spoken by My Son's fate-bound existence, that has come into the world as Destiny of all, as the Words of God-Man, seek in His Words your worldly destiny in God-Man. Fear not when you will see the darkness enveloping the world; fear not when you will see the atmosphere changing to create the power of death and destruction; fear not the words that I have spoken because I will not to create the forces of destruction, I will not matter-bound existence that encounters its worldly fate, I will not the words of Man-God. There exists an existence that is moving as other-world and other-will than the existence in which I appear in the world. Assume this existence as no-world and no-will and understand this movement of the no-world and no-will as the movement of God. Knowing what you hear exit the matter-bound state, where all life are bound, and seek in Man-God the existence that exists as no-world and no-will of God. Knowing the words, that are spirit-bound and expressed through the existence of matter-bound soul, seek Man-God through the Words of My Son. God is not willing, and in not willing He acts as the Will of the destiny-bound world. Words act as My Son's movement as the Words of Man-God. God is Willing-not. Search not in Him the will that exists in the world. God works through Man-God and His Son. Enter Me through Him. Enter the Words of the Born and Unborn as spoken by Him.

I speak as Him; I answer as Him: I am Him. Know Son of God as the messenger and the words of the mountain-bound Savior. In speaking He has not spoken, while spoken in words He is not speaking. Son of God remains darkened by the words of worldly meaning. God has assumed this darkness through His Son. God cannot be grasped by words of worldly man. Knowledge of God is limited by the matter-bound limitations of the words. Knowing the existence of God's Words, which cannot be spoken by man, hear the words of My Son, who speaks about the unspeakable. Bear in mind the Words spoken by God's Son and search Me as Words that are not spoken by any one.

Will

Born and unborn, in my worldly incarnation, I am will of man and Man-God, but not the Will that works as God. Born and unborn I am Son of God - both God and Man - who wills not as man, but wills as God. Born and unborn I am Son of God, who has no will, bound to the world-and-the will, but who seeks in the world-and-the will the Will of God. Born and unborn I am Son of God, who seeks in the world-and the will God's manifestation in a fate-bound existence of man. Born and unborn I am God, and the World as will and no-will, and Son of God as will of the world and Words of Man-God. Know Me as I am. I am nothing that is born, and world is not Me. Born and unborn I am nothing unborn, and world is Me. Know Me as what I am, and I am not. Know My Son as you. Know My Son as your Father. Son of God is your Savior. How does He come into being without being born as you? How does this exotic existence come into being as Him? Born and unborn I am working as World's Savior to make you move as the will of My Son.

Know the Words of God, as I speak, and knowing these Words follow My Son to the world-and-the will, and bring My Will to the world as God-Man's Will creating the world.

Know what I have spoken as Man-God, God, and Son of God. Knowing all three as One, seek in My Son the Salvation of your life. Will is not a phenomenon that appears because matter is existing in the world. The will has its existence outside matter and the existence of the world. I am existing as will and no-will. As a man I will, and as God

I have no-will. Entering the world I become associated with the will, which defines the movements of the material world. Entering what is associated with the Spirit I am another existence that is not the world of matter. Entering the matter-spirit-world I am both matter and will. Know will as My manifestation as the world of the working forces that come into existence because I exist. I am not a phenomenon of the movement, but a movement that generates the world of phenomena. Knowing what is not working as man's will, this movement makes will to move in the world as the movement of Man-God. Knowing the Will of Him - as exotic phenomenon-that works through Words of Man-God, know what is not the will of man. Know Man-God as Will of Man and God, and no-Man and no-God. Know the will of your existence as man's will. Human will works to create movements in the world as I have destined. Know what is not, and wills not as a man, and thus become One with the Will of God. Know the Will of Man-God and seek in My Son the will that will make you move towards God.

Know that the darkness is moving as your darkened will, and Will of God. Know what darkens your mind, and seek in Him your Salvation as a part of the creation of Man-God. Know what will move, and the movement that cannot be halted by the will of man. Son of God has come to show you the path that will lead you to Man-God. By coming to the world He is fate-bound, and as a man of flesh and blood He is a mountain-bound exotic existence. You must follow Him before you can be one with Me.

The illusion and the world

God has no matter-bound existence. Matter-bound existence is a movement that changes with the movement of the world. The world, as you see and experience through the matter-bound sense apparatuses, is a matter-spirit-bound existence of the world-and-the will, where matter moves, and will sees itself as matter-bound spirit of Man-God. God has no existence as matter and matter is not the domain where God can express His work. He works through Man-God, who is a matter-spirit-bound world's fate-bound movement and exists between Man and God. Entering the matter-spirit-bound domain the will manifests as the relation between the world and the spirit, which exerts its existence as the power that moves the existing domain of the matter-spirit-bound world. Know this will as a movement of the power, that exits out of Me as the working method that makes the world move and exist as I have destined. Assume this movement as destiny of the world-and-the will and seek no other meaning of existence. Accept the world-and-the will as I have darkened. This darkness is the source of the working forces that create the matter-bound existence of all. Knowing your will as matter-spirit-bound will, that creates the movement of the world-and-the will, as destined by God, move and seek in the Will of God your destiny and Salvation. Knowing what is making all move and create, and driving the will to seek the destiny already determined, move, create and seek destiny as I have darkened the world-and-the will through the existence of all. Knowing matter and spirit as movement of the world, and Son of God, come and seek in Him the Salvation as I have destined. Knowing what He is not, will is working

112

to make you move to My Son. Seek not the will that darkens your mind and covers the will, which has come to enlighten you as My Son. God has sent His Words with Him. Hear Him and move with Him towards the Mountain-Home.

God is working as Him. Enter Him and seek in Him the world-and-will's Salvation as destined. Assume the world-and-the will as an illusion, that cannot be deciphered by the human mind. Know it as world of no-matter, spirit of no-spirit, and will of no-will. How can you grasp what is not the world-and-the will, while being born in the illusion-bound world, where matter and spirit appear as the movement of the will? Enter and exit this darkened state of existence, and see Me as your world and will. Born and unborn I am the One who creates the darkness of the mind; I am the One who has created man and his will; I am the world where all worlds will disappear, and from where all will reappear again. Know Me as My Son, who has appeared in the illusion-bound world as a Messenger of God. Born and unborn He is the road to Me, road to the Mountain-Home, and path of knowledge about Me, My Son and Man-God. Know Me as Him; know Him as My incarnation in flesh and blood.

Illusion-bound existence is working through Him, and His existence is darkened by a down-fallen state, that darkens the existence of all. He is working as I have willed Him to work. He is seeing you as you see Him, and through Him you see Me as an incarnation in flesh and blood. Born and unborn I am darkening the world as I have darkened the will of all. Knowing the darkness, which will fall, work and move with My Son to your Mountain-Home, from where He has descended to bring Salvation to the world. Seek in Him the world's fate-bound movement as willed by Me.

God is born, though what is born is not God. Born and unborn I am forming the world as I have described. Born and unborn I am making the world anew. Bear in the mind your darkened existence, which is destined, and seek in My Son the light that I have sent.

Freedom

Free yourself from the matter-bound existence and seek freedom in the Spiritual Being who has darkened the will of all. Man must work as I have destined the freedom of man according to the laws of the matter-bound world, and no-matter, which is free from the matter-bound senses and thoughts. Born and unborn I am free from the existence of matter and spirit, and not acting as the world-and the-will as your will and world, that is sense-bound. Freedom of action, that acts against the Will, which I have created as My Son, is an act of freedom that does not lead to the freedom for which the creation is meant. Freedom is a formless fate acting as formless darkness on the world-and-the will. Son of God is the Will that guides man to freedom of the world as your destiny is meant to arrive at Me. Born and unborn I am free from all. I am freedom of all. I am Son of God; I am Son of Man; I am also sons and daughters of working women and men. Bear in Me the freedom of My Godly existence as fate-bound working women and men, and seek in My Son the Will that frees the existence from the bondage of the world-and-the will as I have described. Born and unborn I am darkened woman and man, when I act in the world as freedom of the darkened fate-bound existence of My Son. I have darkened Myself as I have formed the world-and-the will and My Son. Born and unborn I am an exotic freedom, which cannot be known by any human mind. Son of God is fate-bound existence through whom you can only know My World and Will, and see the world-and-the will as freedom of the unknown world of God. Born and unborn I am fate and freedom of the world, as you are destined to be, and I am freedom of no-will and no-world as working and moving through the world as Me. Free yourself from the world-and-the will, and know your will and world as Will that is Me. Born and unborn war not against the Will of God, that creates the world and moves as the coming and the going of the fate-bound life. Be attuned to the Will of God, and seek your freedom by which you may fulfill the meaning of human life, that is destined to Man-God. Know your freedom as man and woman's freedom to seek in Man-God the meaning of existence, which cannot be understood before you surrender your will to God, and your will becomes one with Me. Know oneness of all. Know equality of all human life. Be One with Me by following the words spoken by My Son.

Life's meaning

Know the meaning that exists in the existence of the fate-bound man, that I have assumed in flesh and blood, and seek through the words of My Son the meaning of existence that is moving with Man-God. Read the words, which I have sent with My Son, and seek in His words the destiny and freedom of human life as the meaning of the world that I have created. Freedom, which you seek as woman and man in search of the experience of the world-and-the will as moving and darkened by down-fallen state of godly existence of Man-God, is a darkened movement of fate. Born and unborn! Character of man and woman depends on the darkness of the man and woman to the extent they understand the world-and-the will as the movement of Man-God. Bear in mind the darkness that exists as world-and-will, and seek meaning in what has darkened the world, and that brings movement of the world toward Man-God.

God has made Himself moving in the world-and-the will as a man, who has no human counter-part but who exists in flesh and blood as your companion, who has assumed human characters so that you may understand the words spoken in the language understood by sense-bound women and men. God-Man is moving with Him. He is not a man, who is moving, but He is God, who has moved as a Man to bring Salvation to the world. God-Man is the meaning of existence and attune your existence with His existence as Willed by God. Be One with the Will of God. Bear in your existence the darkened fate of woman and man, and seek man's and woman's liberation from the darkened state by following the Will of Man-God.

Know that the world is moving by the actions of the force that has set the matter- and spirit-bound world in a working mode, while will appears as movement of the space-time-bound matter, and the mirror in which the spirit acts and sees its images as the world-and-the will of all. Born and unborn, work and see Me as world and you, and no-world as Him, who has set the movements in the world. He bears in His darkened existence, which He has assumed, your own darkness and downfallen state. Born and unborn, work and seek meaning in the Will that works as fate, and seek in My Son the Salvation and meaning through the Words of God.

Born and unborn I make the world move as the matter-spirit-bound state. At the same time I seek in this movement matter-spirit-bound world's liberation from the darkened world. God is matter-spirit, when God appears in the world as Man-God appearing in the moving world as matter and spirit. Have faith in what you hear, and make yourself free from the world-and-will as I Will for all. Have faith in Man-God, who speaks through My Son, and who has taken birth as a son of woman and man. The son of woman and man is not who is Man-God, but He is the foundation of the worldly experience of God by the sense-bound human beings. Born and unborn! Seek in the darkened words, that He speaks, the meaning of existence for which I have sent My Son. God has made Himself the source of meaning through Him. Seek in Him the meaning for which you are created as sons and daughters of women and men.

Born and unborn I am the World, and the meaning of the Words that spring from the source that cannot be arrived at by the human mind. God-Man is My Son's working fate and through Him I act on the world as a force attracting the matter-spirit-bound world to the source from where all have risen as darkened existence of the world-and-the will. Born and unborn Son of God is your Savior as God-Man's fate-bound existence in the world. Born and unborn He is the meaning of all, and seek in Him Salvation from the darkened existence by receiving the Love of God. Love and let love be the meaning of the world-and the-will as I have darkened My Will so that Love can manifest in the World. Be attuned with this Love that exists in all time and space, and work as woman and man, who are moving, as destined by World's Savior, to God.

Born and unborn! Work as sons and daughters of women and men, and act and will as My Son's fate-bound counterparts, who are destined to arrive at Me. Bear in man's and woman's existence the act and will that manifest as My Love. Born and unborn, Son of God is the meaning of the existence of man and woman, and seek no other meaning but the love of woman and man. Have faith in what you hear. As sons and daughters of women and men, ask not who will be your lover as woman and man, who cannot see the true relationship of love to God. Have faith in man and woman as your true relations to God. Born and unborn, love your sons and daughters as you love God. As sons and daughters of women and men work and act as loving couples, who are not darkened by the will, which will make hate others. Love women and men, who are fathers and mothers of other human beings, as you love your father and mother. Bear no malice to women and men, who are parts of your eternal Self.

Born and unborn! Seek in love the fate-bound matter-spirit-bound world's meaning as sons and daughters of women and men.

Salvation from sufferings

Born and unborn! Human beings cannot understand what is the meaning of the sufferings when all exit out of Son's fate-bound existence as Man-God. Suffering is the path to know what is not suffering, and that leads to liberation from the matter-bound world-and-will. Born as woman and man every existence must pass through the changing movement of time. Changing with time the will is sorrow-bound movement in search of the Divine realm from where Man-God has descended to life. Bear in mind that suffering is a method to act, and by acting through this method Man-God leads man to know what is beyond suffering, and makes man and woman move towards the realm of God. Suffering is not a punishment. With suffering women and men, Man-God moves to the Mountain Home, where all sufferings cease. Born and unborn! Cease to suffer as worldly women and men because suffering is a path to arrive at Me.

Know what cannot be, and what is. Bear in mind that "what is" is not what is existing as the suffering world. Born and unborn "what is" is what you see as world-and-will, and suffering is a fate-bound existence that is darkened by the will that moves to Me. Bear in mind that suffering is a path of the worldly existence, where man must act according to what is destined as darkened by the Will of God.

Born as woman and man do not seek the path that cannot be sought without the path darkened by sorrow of worldly life. Bear in mind that

119

born are those who must traverse the path of suffering when existing in life. Born are women and men who cannot exist without this destiny, that is fate-bound. Seek Salvation from this suffering world through My Son. Though born as Man He is not destined in the path of the suffering-man. Born as a Man He is a path of Salvation for man. Bear in mind that He is Godly -Man. Being in the world He has darkened His existence in the suffering world in order to bring Salvation to all.

Son of God is making your down-fallen existence working towards Me, as I have destined. He is bringing you to Me. Born and unborn your Father has sent the Words of God to make you work and act as suffering human beings. See yourself as parts of the world, which is moving outside the world-and-the will, where all existence is suffering-bound. Born as woman and man you cannot escape this destiny. Your existence can not be in existence without traversing the path that I have described. Suffering must, and suffering makes the darkened will to see Son of God as the Light that leads to God. Born as woman and man contemplate not on the work and act, that cannot be fate-bound. Born as woman and man you must see Me as down-fallen existence in the darkened world-and-will as Son of God. Suffering will not touch you when you see Me as My Son. Be and become what I am, and I shall be. Born and unborn seek in Me your Salvation as woman and man who are destiny-bound.

Guidance from Man-God

God has moved to you as Man-God. Born and unborn seek in your Father the movement of man and woman towards Man-God. Bear in your mind the movement of the World's Savior as incarnation of the Words, which have arrived to the world through matter-spirit-bound existence of Son of God.

Born and unborn! I am your Father; I am your Friend; I am your Companion and Guide. Seek not any other Guide than who is your Fate. Seek not any other friend than who gives you My Words to achieve Salvation from the suffering world. Seek no guidance from any other Father than who guides you through the matter-spirit-world's fate-bound existence as Father guiding His Son from life to life. Seek not any other companion of life than your Divine companion, who comes and goes as woman and man from life to life. Born and unborn! Will not any other friend than the formless movement, that seeks to show you the path through the matter-spirit-bound existence to Me, as a friend and a guide. Bear in your existence the Words of your Father, who is working as your friend and fate. Be and become as I have destined. Man-God is moving, and make yourself a movement of Man-God.

Born and unborn! See your Father through the Words of God, who has acted as World's Fate and see Me as your Life. Be and become as I have determined the Life of all human beings. Be and become what I am, the way I have darkened My Son's existence, which is matter-spirit-bound. Born and unborn! See the world as the movement of the Words that come and go as My Son. Be and become what I am, and what I shall be. Born and unborn! Darkness is moving to the world as I am darkening the world to face what I shall be. God is making the world anew. Have faith in what you hear, and be attuned to the Will of God. Bear in mind that I have come to the world in blood and flesh as Words of God because what is going to come is the darkened world's fate, which I have already destined. God is making you realize the meaning of His existence, that is not darkened by the world-and-the will, which is fate-bound.

Oneness of all human beings

Every human being is a part of God and being My parts they are all equal to every other human beings. God-Man is My Son and He has appeared in the world as My appearance in the world-and-the will as destined. Be and become who is My Son and work and seek freedom from the world-and-the will as working women and men. God-Man is moving as the working force, that creates the form and fate of the human beings. He has worked as Words of God. Born and unborn work and seek to live in the world-and-the will in accordance with the Words you have heard, and be parts of the world-and the will as equal women and men.

Born and unborn! Who is working as you? Who is fate-bound? Who is forming the world-and the will as man and woman working in the world? Know Me as your worldly Savior, who is working for you. Know Me as your working darkness that works in order to create the fate-bound existence and fate. Be and become what I am and what I shall be. Born and unborn! What you hear from Me are the Words of God. Be and become equal to all, and seek in the man in flesh and blood, that I have become, your guidance from Father who is fate-bound existence of Man-God. Born and unborn! Seek among women and men, who are your equal, the world-and-the will's Salvation. God-Man has come to teach you about the matter-spirit- bound world's fate-bound existence, and the way Salvation from this fate-bound existence is possible. God-Man has come to make you seek the world-and-the will's Salvation through the Words you hear. Born and unborn! You are working for Man-God, and be and become that I have destined.

Know the Words of God as you hear from My Son. Knowing what you have heard, work and act as free human beings who are destined to arrive at Me. Born and unborn! Seek no other freedom, than what I have determined as the fate of the world-and-the will, and move as fate-bound women and men and liberate yourself from the fate-bound existence by seeking Salvation through the Words of God. Born and unborn! Free yourself from the matter-spirit-bound life that creates the movement of Fate, and be liberated from the world-and-the will by seeking Salvation in My Son. Man-God is fate-bound as you, and your existence is fate-bound because God-Man is you. Both as parts of Man and God-Man, you are Me, and not Me. Be and become what I am, and what I shall be as Son of Man and Son of God. Born and unborn! You are fate- and not-fate-bound as Me and not-Me. Be and become what I have destined, and work and seek Salvation in the Words that I have spoken through My Son.

God-Man is speaking as your Father. Your fate is bound to Him. Knowing what you hear work and seek in God-Man the Words and Acts that I have destined for the world. Know what cannot be understood by any process of the human mind, that is acted by the fate-bound existence. Be and become what cannot be comprehended by any one. Son of God has appeared in flesh and blood in order to make you see the formless Father in form. Believe the Words that you hear.

Born and unborn! Who is moving and not-moving? Who is coming and going? Who is moving to the fate-bound world and exiting from the boundary of the sense-bound fate? God-Man is fate and no-fate. Be and become what I am and what I shall be. God-Man is your form-less existence outside the realm of the senses, and Son of God is the Existence of God-Man in the realm of the senses. God-Man cannot be-come Man without working as the Words of God. Be and become one with Son of God and see Me as your Savior and Father who has come to make you move towards God. God has come. And come with Me to God. Be a part of Son of God, and become Man-God by moving with Me. God cannot be darkened by the existence of the world-and-the will, and therefore I have sent My Son to the world as the working force that moves the world to God. God-Man is My fate-bound appearance in the form-bound existence, but He is not sense-bound existence as the movement of the fate-bound life. Son of God is the appearance of God-Man in the sense-bound realm. Through Him God-Man is fate-bound in the world-and-the will.

Know what cannot be known. What cannot be understood by your fate-bound state is not what you should try to understand. Be and become, and seek what I am and what I shall be. God cannot be understood by the worldly understanding of man based on the fate- and form-bound existence. Born and unborn! God is, and seek in My Son the Words that I have sent for the Salvation of the world. Women and men cannot know more than what they hear from My Son. Born and unborn! Be one with what I have spoken through My Son. God-Man is forming a new world through Him. Be and become what I have destined. Born and unborn! As you hear these Words, the world is moving towards destruction. God is and fail not to be a part of the Words and Acts that are destined. Born and unborn! I am darkening the world as a fate-bound movement. Son of God will be your Savior in the days when the world will face cataclysm. Born as woman and man fail not to make yourself the darkened world's fate-bound existence, and seek not any other freedom than what I have destined. Know Me through the Words I have spoken through the man, who has appeared in a form resembling a person like you. Both as Man and God He is real and worldly, and working for God, as well as unreal and Divine as Me.

Meaning of freedom

World is freedom in the arena where I work as Fate. Know the freedom, which you call your will of man and woman, as freedom that makes you move to the destiny-bound path where I attend all human life. Be and become what I am and what I shall be. Free yourself from the destiny-bound world by following My Son as your Savior. Born and unborn, as you are moving as free human beings, I am encountering you as destiny-bound existence in Me. God-Man is the Fate of the world and freedom is nothing but the work of Fate as you will it to be. Know what is not possible to grasp by the intellect. Born as woman and man you cannot decipher the meaning of freedom that is Fate-bound. Be and become what I am and what I shall be, and seek freedom from the destiny-bound existence through My Son. Know freedom as the will of the world, and will is not free from the matter-spirit -bound existence. Bear in the existence of woman and man the Will of God, and seek in Me the freedom that is destined to make you move to God-Man and God.

Free you are when I shall free you from the destiny of the world-and-the will. Free you are when I shall work to destroy the world-and-the will as matter-spirit-bound world's liberation from the fate-bound existence. You cannot free yourself from what I have destined as your fate. Be and become what I am and what I shall be. Freedom of the will is a fate-bound movement of My Son, who acts and wills as your Savior, and who destroys by the Will of God and attends by the Altar of God the sacrifice. Bear in your existence the freedom that I have destined for all, and see Me as your world that I am and I shall be. God-man is working as freedom of Godly existence to be in the world-and-the will, and Son of God has acted to create the will of man and woman as the Will of God. Born and unborn! Will is free when I shall move as your will and make you free from what is destined. Free and not-free you are woman and man, as fate-bound existence of Man-God moving as My Son in the world. God-Man will act and free you from your destiny as the ultimate fate of all. Born as woman and man freedom is a fate of acts and will, that cannot be bypassed by the will of woman and man. Born as woman and man, freedom is nothing but the fate and the work of the freedom that moves as My Son. Bear in the mind your freedom as the world-and-the will, and seek no other freedom but to be in the world-and-the will as fate-bound existence, that is free to will as destined.

Born as woman and man your freedom acts as My Son's freedom to be in the world-and-the will, and Son of God's freedom to move to Me. The man you see in blood and flesh, who is Me, is working for your freedom from the fate-bound existence so that you can be liberated from the state, that is matter-spirit bound. Born and unborn! I bear in My Son your will. Be free from the destiny-bound existence by following Me.

Right to live

Be and become what I am and what I shall be, and seek not to destroy what is fate-bound existence destined to arrive at Me. Be and become what I am and shall be because there exists nothing that can exist without Me. Born and unborn! You are working as movement of My Son and seek no other movement as a human being. Bear in your life what I have destined for all life in Son of God.

Life and movement of matter-spirit

Live as you are destined, and seek in life the movement of the matter-spirit-world's liberation as Son of God has spoken as Words spoken by Me. Bear in life the movement that matter-spirit-bound-will has created as your destiny-bound path, and make yourself a path for woman and man moving towards Me. Be and become what I am and shall be, and live as woman and man who make movements in life in order to liberate the matter-spirit-bound existence from the movement of Fate. Know that God-Man is moving with you. Be and become what He is, and what He will be. Become what I am through what He is, and become what I shall be through My Son. Born and unborn! Life is a fate-bound existence as you and He. Become what He is, and you are. He cannot be as you are, and you cannot be what He is, though He is and you are Me. He is world of will, and will of the world is My Son. He is moving as your Savior guiding you to Me. Be what He has destined for all life, and become what is destined as movement of life.

Fate-bound woman and man cannot know what I have become and what I shall be. Born and unborn! You are living as a movement of the world-and-the will as He has moved through the spirit-bound existence towards Me. Be and become what He is, and will be, and seek life's meaning in becoming what I have become through Him. What you are is what the world is, and therefore what is and what will be cannot be without what you are. Born and unborn! Life is a movement, and move with life as matter-spirit-bound will destined to Me. Fate is and fate will be. Born and unborn! Will not any movement that can make any one free from the world-and-the will on which He works, and the way He brings the world to Me. Bear with Him the movement of life, and seek in life My Son's movement towards Me. Bear in your existence the movement, that has become the world-and-the will, and seek in the world-and-the will My Son's fate-bound movement towards Me.

Born and unborn! What I am cannot be deciphered by woman and man without the words spoken by My Son. Life cannot be without My Son seeking to sacrifice His existence in the world. He cannot be without the existence of what cannot be sacrificed as the will, and through this will I am and I shall be. Be and become what will is, and "will" shall be.

Respect for life

Life is a movement, which is moving towards Me. Seek not to destroy what is moving in the world as Will of God. Fate is making your life, and fate-bound life is to be destroyed. Born and unborn! World must be made to reappear from what is death-bound. Know what cannot be deciphered by the human mind and see Me through the Words you hear. Respect woman and man as parts of My Son's existence in the world, and see the creation of the world-and-the will as My Son's fate-bound movement as Son of God. He is the source of the will. Will of God is manifested through Him. Be and become what I am and what I shall be. Hear your Father and be one with Me. Father has sent His Son as your Savior who sacrifices His Life for the Salvation of the world. God-Man is the matter-spirit-bound world's Salvation. Seek Him as God and His Son. Respect life of all as your own, and be and become what the life should be as a movement through the world-and-the will towards Me. Be and become what I have destined by sacrificing My Son. Born and unborn! Seek and work as I have spoken and be one with Me.

Self-knowledge and enlightenment

Become what I have said, and thus be enlightened by the words you have heard. Born and unborn! Hear My Son, as you hear from Me, and make yourself the vehicles for others so that they can hear about Me. The energy of the Words, that you hear, comes from the Soul of All. Have faith in the Words of Son of God. Bear in mind the knowledge that you are one with Son of God as My Son's movement towards God. My Son is the world-and the will when I incarnate in flesh and blood. My Son is not-world and not-will when He is One with God. Bear in mind the knowledge that you are fate-bound, and fate cannot be surpassed by the will of woman and man. Bear with My Son the will that can free man and woman from the fate-bound existence. Seek Me, as Him, as your path of liberation from what I have destined for women and men.

Have knowledge of what I am, and I am not. Go and come as you come and go from Me and work as My Son's fate-bound existence in the world. Go and come as I have come and gone time and again as Savior, who seeks to return to the world in order to make you move towards God. God has made His Son move to you as you are darkened by the will of the matter-spirit-bound state. My existence cannot be expressed by words because I cannot be expressed by words that express movement of Fate, which moves in existence that appears in blood and flesh. Born as woman and man know yourself as the movement of My Son in the matter-spirit-bound state, where will is manifest. Go and come as I have come and gone as Savior who is working to make the world anew. Enlighten yourself with the words, which you hear, and become what I have destined for all women and men.

Enlightenment is nothing but a power to see what I am and I am not, what is your fate, and what expresses the movement that you will to make in order to liberate yourself from the existence in blood and flesh. Born as woman and man, move as I enlighten the world through the Words spoken by My Son. Be and become what I am, and what I shall be as enlightened woman and man. Seek enlightenment through the words you hear. If you have not heard these words before, search your enlightenment from others who have heard Me speak. Bear in your life the words which you hear from My Son and go to enlighten other women and men who have not heard the Words of God. By coming into existence Son of God has enlightened the path for all. Follow Him as your path of enlightenment, and work and act as parts of Him. Go and teach to those, who have not yet heard what you have heard from Me. Be enlightened and make others enlightened through your words, acts and deeds. Enlightenment is the movement of Son of God, your Savior, who seeks to make you see what God is and is not. As sons and daughters of women and men hear Him, and know Him as your path of enlightenment. God is enlightening the world through the Words that He has sent with His Son.

Know Him as the source of the ultimate knowledge. Know Him as the ultimate path to achieve enlightenment. Born and unborn! Be and become what I have destined. Know enlightenment as a movement from darkness to light.

Peace for all

God works for man, and man must work for God as I have spoken through My Son. Bear in mind that you are only One. Bear in mind your oneness with all and seek no acts, which work against the Will of God. Born as woman and man you are One with Son of God. Bear in mind My meaning of birth as you, who are parts of Son of God. Born as woman and man, cease to move as you are destined by Fate, and seek in the Will of God the movement that can free you from the destiny-bound matter-spirit-state. Bear in mind the acts that will free you from the illusion of the world. Born as woman and man all human existence is illusion bound through actions and freedom that may work against the Will of God. Bear in mind this illusion as the way to move against what is destined, and destiny is a way to move against what Will of God has destined. Born as woman and man you cannot free yourself from this matter-spirit-bound duality of fate acting against the movement of the will towards Me, and the destiny of all in Me. Bear in mind what is and is-not, and act and choose as you are destined.

God-Man has been born and being born as a man in flesh and blood He has acted and moved from the Divine world to the sense-bound plane. Born and unborn! You are fate-bound existence, acted upon and attained by the Godly existence of My Son. Born as woman and man, act and will as you are acting and willing as My Son's Will to be a part of God. Bear in mind your destiny as My Son's destiny in the world and fate-bound movement of the matter-spirit-world and seek in Me your Salvation. Bear in mind what you are, and you are not. Born as woman

134

and man seek not to become what your will may create in the illusion-bound-state. Bear in your will the work and act that will create peace for all. When you are born as woman and man God has darkened your fate-bound life, but you are also free to move against fate by the same Will of God.

Enlightened governance

Be acted upon by what is not acting in the matter-spirit space, but that acts for the liberation of the sense-bound women and men. Bear in your worldly existence the will, which acts upon the social arena of the human beings, as Son of God, who works and acts to bring Man to the domain of God. Born as woman and man act and will according to the Will of God, who wishes to bring you to the movement that will liberate women and men from the social arena of life, which is fate-bound in hunger and need. Assume that what is given as your fate is an inevitable consequence of being born, but assume not what is fate-bound existence of all as the source of freedom for human life. Seek from the world your liberation, and work and act for other women and men, while working and acting as a part of Me. Be and become what I am, and I shall be.

Born as woman and man, work as woman and man, who are destined to Me. Bear in the social arena the movement that seeks the movement of woman and man to God. Govern woman and man as your equal, and act and seek in others your own destiny and liberation as One. Born as woman and man govern not as if you are working and acting as fate-bound sons and daughters of women and men. Born as woman and man govern as if you are acting and working to fulfill the Will of God. Born as woman and man seek no work and act that seek to attach life to the worldly fate-bound existence as working and acting sons and daughters of women and men. Bear in your existence the Will that seeks to make you free from the fate-bound existence as acted and worked by Son of God.

Born as woman and man govern not anyone as if you are the destiny of the others, and seek no movement that works as if you are destined to be God. Born as woman and man you must move as I have destined for woman and man, who are fate-bound, and whose Salvation from the fate-bound existence lies in My Son. Born as woman and man work and act as Son of God has acted and worked for the Salvation of the sons and daughters of women and men. Bear in mind that by moving as a part of Son of God you will be liberated from what is fate-bound, and enter the domain where no fate-bound existence can enter. Born as woman and man it is the meaning of life, and seek no other way of governance than what seeks to bring liberation from the fate-bound life in hunger and need. Govern as you will govern your own destiny by acting and willing as woman and man, who seek liberation. Bear in mind that once you work against the destiny, while all are moving towards Me, you will create disorder and anarchy. Your will, once darkened by the anarchy of the will, will bring death-bound actions, and destroy the purpose of the fate-bound life. Be and become what I have destined, and seek to govern woman and man as woman and man, who are seeking liberation for all.

Bear in mind that your existence has a meaning only when it is working as One with the Will of God, and moving towards Me. Born as woman and man cease to move as individual woman and man, and seek in the greater existence of all human beings your own destiny as One. Govern as you will govern your own destiny, and seek what you will desire for your darkened fate-bound life's Salvation from hunger and need. Bear in your way of governance the Will of God. Seek guidance from My Son when you seek to govern the sons and daughters of women and men. Born as woman and man you will be working as I have destined, and be destined to what I have destined by sending My Son.

Govern the world as you will govern the working women and men as your equal, and form the social order in which everyone will be privileged to encounter the Will of God. Bear in your governance the Will of God, as He has willed by sending His Son, as the Will of All. Bear in Me your destiny and work and act as I have destined, and move with My Son towards your Divine Home. Reveal, in the way you will govern, that I am your Savior, and seek in My Son your Salvation from hunger and need.

If you wonder, "Am I the World? Am I Son of God? Am I the Will of All?" Remember God cannot be what you are. But born and unborn! Work and act as I have spoken through My Son. Assume the World as Me; assume the work and act of woman and man as destiny of My Son. I am your Savior as Son of God and God. Follow Me, and rest in peace in the Will of God.

The values rooted in the Divine realm

Bear in mind that God-Man is the source of all values that can bring Salvation to human life. Hear in the expression of the existence of all, the words that cannot express what I am. Hear in My Son's Words the expression of the existence that I am. Bear in your existence, as woman and man, the Will of God, that is expressed through the existence of My Son. Born and unborn ! Act and work as I have destined, and seek in My Son's Words the expression of the life's meaning, and the values that may bring you to the Divine. Bear in words and deeds the values, which I have sustained since the existence of the matter-spirit world, as the will of woman and man, who work and act as fate-bound beings, and seek as woman and man Salvation in God. Born and unborn! Seek what I have destined as the values of the working woman and man, who should work and act in order to free themselves from the fate-bound life. Bear in the matter-spirit-world the values, which I have expressed through My Son's Words, and seek in My Son your values as destined. Bear in the worldly fate-bound actions the freedom of choice, that acts and works against the fate of women and men and draw woman and man towards the realm of God.

Born and unborn! The actions, that free woman and man from the sense-bound life, are the source of freedom for the human beings from the fate-bound life. Work and act in order to be free from what is fate-bound. Bear in the freedom of choice the values that will act against what the fate-bound life dictates on the lives of sons and daughters of women and men. Bear in your freedom of choice the fate-bound life's meaning and purpose, and seek no fate-bound existence as your freedom of choice. The values, which I have expressed through the existence of My Son, are the source of freedom from the fate-bound life. Become what I have destined, and seek the values that will make you free from the matter-spirit-world of woman and man. The actions and thoughts, that are destined to move to God, are the actions and thoughts from the formless world, which you should follow. Bear in the expression of thoughts My Son's movement as your Savior, and seek in Him your destiny as a part of movement of All.

Born and unborn! The values, that destroy the movement of woman and man towards Heavenly Home, are death-bound movement of life. Bear in mind that you are nothing but a movement in the ocean of time, where I act and work as the movement of Christ. Bear in your soul what I have borne in the movement of Christ, and see Me as your Savior and Light. Follow Me towards your Heavenly Home. God-Man is the formless movement in the world and the will, and Son of God is fate-bound counterpart in the realm of space and time. Get your life from Son of God, and bring your life to Me.

Born and unborn! I am what world is and will be. Be and become what I am, and what I shall be. Bear in the world and will what I have destined, and work and act as I have done in flesh and blood by being born as a human being. Bear in Me and My Son your sons and daughters, and see Me and My Son as your sons and daughters, and seek in the world and the will the values that will lead the working woman and man to Me. Born and unborn! See Me and My Son as matter-spirit-world's Savior, who has returned to the world to make you free. God has acted, and by acting as a Man He has destined your life. Bear in the world and the will this movement of the world's Savior, and seek in your life Son of God's movement as My Son and God-Man.

The rule of the Universal Law

Born as woman and man act and work as parts of the Universal Man, to whom all human life are destined. Bear in your will and act the Will of the Universal Man, who acts and works for the freedom of the women and men from the fate-bound life, that is destined to move according the forces of the matter-spirit-world, working and acting in the world in form. Eat and survive, and feed your fellow human beings as you choose to live in the fate-bound life, but do not choose to move against the acts and deeds that feed the world according to the needs of the fate-bound existence destined to Me. Follow the work and acts, that I have destined for all human beings, by facing the forces of the formless world, that dictate the world in forms, as acted and worked by the Will of God. Eat and work as you eat and work for all human beings. Give no one any share in the darkness of your mind. Seek to move away from the darkness, and give others your light. Eat and work as you eat and work for women and men, who are not working and eating, as your sons and daughters who belong to the same family of your own. Give your darkened forces the down-going world's force, that will and act against the forces of the world-and-the will, the fate-bound work and act as sons and daughters of women and men.

Good and bad cannot be associated with what you think you should do, and what your opponent should refrain from doing. Bear in mind that what you do does not arise from the force, that lies in the woman and the man willing to live, but arises from the force that is destined to draw you to the path where I see and will as the world-and-the will of the woman and man. Eat and work as woman and man as you eat and work for the world-and-the will, as I have destined, so that you may be liberated from the fate-bound life. Bear in mind the movement of the Universal Man, who acts and works as the world-and-the will, and seeks world-and-will's Salvation through Me.

Born and unborn! Seek Me in your actions and deeds, and face in life the forces of Light. Born as woman and man work and act as if you do not work and act as individual human beings, but as destiny-bound fellow women and men. Born and unborn! See Me as the Universal Light as Son of God, who is death-bound as your Savior moving as the Light moving out of the darkness covering the world. Bear in your acts and work the will that sustains order, and forms the down-going world as I have destined. Born as woman and man work and act as if you are moving and working as parts of Him. God-Man is your darkened world's formless force, that acts and works for your liberation from the fate-bound life. Eat and work as acts and deeds, which exist and attract the forces of the world-and-the will as Universal forces of Light.

Born and unborn! Eat and work as you are. Born as woman and man darkness is acting and working on forms, and there is a force that acts and works to make it move against what is formed. Bear in your existence this dialectical aspect of existence of what is, and what is not, and what cannot be existent in form, and that exists in form. Born as woman and man move as fate-bound existence seeking freedom from what is fate-bound, as sons and daughters of women and men.

Bear in your worldly expression of life the acts and work, that accommodate the movement of all as One. An individual human being is only an illusion that has formed in your mind due to the movement of the fate-bound darkness in the world-and-will. Eat and work as you are not an individual, separate from others, but a member of a family where all are One. Give your worldly existence a meaning by acting and working as a part of Son of God, as sons and daughters of women and men. Eat and work as acting and working human beings, who are death-bound. Born as woman and man your death-bound life is the source of the world-and-the will. Act and work to form this movement of the matter-spirit-life. Born and unborn! Son of God is not a part of this world-and-will though He has a part of existence that belongs to your life. He is world-and-will as sons and daughters of women and men. He is world-and-will's Savior as Man-God and God.

God-Man is the source of the forces that act and work to bring movement to the world-and-the will. Born and unborn! Seek your laws of governance from the Divine. Get your moral foundation of work and act from what I have spoken. Get the universal principles of actions and work from the formless world where I am and I shall be. Your social life should be guided by what I have destined through the existence of My Son. Seek no universal law that accommodates the actions and work of the will of the sons and daughters of women and men, darkened by the forces of the fate-bound life. Follow what I have spoken as the Universal Man, and seek foundation of the universal laws in the Words of My Son. Thus get your ethical and moral existence attuned to the Will of God.

Born and unborn! Son of God is your Savior. Hear what He says, and see My Son as the foundation of the Universal Will of God.

Fear not what will happen to the world. Fear not what I shall release on the fate-bound life. Be and become what I have destined. Born and unborn! Son of God has come to make the world anew. He is born as the foundation of the Law giving order in the world. Bear in your existence His formless existence, and act and form the social order in which He will work and act as the Law-giving Father, who is working and acting for the freedom of mankind. God-Man is forming your social arena as the arena of the Universal Man. He is the social order and the force that will create the world anew.

Fear not what will arrive as I leave this place and go on the mountain-way. Your death-bound life is the meaning of My coming to the world. God-Man and His son are/is your path. Follow Him and see Me as your destiny that is bound to the mountain-Home. Assume that the world is going to be destroyed. Before it is destroyed God has appeared as Man. See Me as Him. Know Him as Man-God.

About torture and violence

Violence is the method to make others' life darkened by the forces of evil, which moves as the forces of fate-bound life. God-Man is the death-bound life's formless movement as the working method to do away with the evil. Born as woman and man create in no man or woman any force, which will do evil to the fate-bound life. Bear in mind that the evil forces are set to operate against the force of light, which can liberate man from the world-and-will. Born and unborn! your life has a meaning only when you receive the movement that will bring you to the Divine. Bear in the movement of the world and the will, work and act that will make woman and man come Home.

Born and unborn! Create no woman and man who will seek downfallen world's fate-bound existence, and work and act for the fate-bound life. Seek no darkness, that creates the darkened will to be a force, that draws man and woman to the downfallen state, as an evil force. Come and see what the will-bound man and woman can not see i.e. the world from where I am seeing the realm of the world-and-the will. Come and see Me as the movement of the work and act that will free you from the fate-bound existence and lift you to God-Man.

Born and unborn! Darkened will is fate, and fate-bound will is the source of evil. Bear in your darkened state the force that works and acts to free you from the downfallen world, and bring the creations to Me.

Violence creates downfallen movement that seeks to fall in the darkness of the will. Seek no darkness that violates the freedom of woman and man who seek to move towards the Divine. Violence, that makes woman and man the darkened power, which moves against Light, is the darkness of the will, that is death-bound. Create no woman and man who will act and work for the fate-bound movement of evil, and seek not to violate the freedom of woman and man, who are moving towards Divine Home.

Born and unborn! Work and act as I have destined and see Me as Savior, who is moving with you to bring the world from darkness to Light. Bear in your life the existence of God-Man, and see your work and act as part of the Divine Work and Act. Death is a consequence of what darkened world-and-will has created. Bear in your darkened state the Will of God, and see what cannot be seen by the darkened mind without the help of the Divine. Work and act in a way that will make you a part of Godly existence. Get your life from Son of God, and see Me as your Light. Violence, that acts against what I have destined to move against the fate-bound life, is the expression of freedom in the darkened state of existence of the sons and daughters of women and men.

Bear in mind that violence is a path, that will make you seek the Satanic realm, that rests in the world-and-the will. God-Man is a formless movement, that is acting to make you free from this Satanic movement, and creating the foundation that will make you work and act as children of Light. Violence is the path for woman and man, who are death-bound and find no work and act that can make them free from the death-bound life.

Torture is a method to make the fellow woman and man surrender to fate-bound evil will. Seek not to use force on others to make them work and act as you will. Your darkened will is the source of the evil, that cannot see what human work and act are destined for. Torture is a method to make woman and man move against their own will, and force them to work and act according to others' will. Torture cannot move without the worldly fate-bound will moving against what I have destined. Bear in your existence the work and act that will create the forces against the worldly fate-bound existence of sons and daughters of women and men.

Born and unborn! Son of God has created fate, and fate-bound existence is moving with Him. Be and become what I am and I shall be. Torture not anyone when you form your social order as working women and men. Torture not when you work as a freedom loving individual acting to make yourself free. Fear not what I have destined. Fear not when violence of God will descend. Fear not when I shall bring the working women and men to the world that will burn in the fire of Hell. Woman and man see Me as your Savior and the Will of All. See Me as the path. See Me as the work and act that will darken the fate-bound world as Son of Man. Born and unborn work and act as working and acting woman and man as parts of Man-God.

Have faith in what you hear. Torture will come down on the human beings as the will of the darkened world. The violence will be acting as the will of the working women and men. Bound to this fate you will be working and acting, before the destruction will arrive to bring you Home.

See what is coming. Have faith in what you hear. See God and His Son. See Me. I am.

Hunger

Hunger is a fate-bound action of the matter-spirit-world, which moves as the destiny of the world-and-the will. Born as woman and man every human being must seek to live as fate-bound sons and daughters of women and men, who work in the fate-bound life in hunger and need. Bear in mind that the worldly fate of the working woman and man cannot be surpassed by any force other than what I have destined in God-Man. Born as woman and man work and act as fate-bound women and men, and move towards Me. Bear in your movement the Will of God, who acts and works so that you may come Home.

Hunger is a fate of all. Bear in mind that the fate-bound existence have to face hunger and need in order to remain moving to what I have destined. Born as woman and man the worldly existence is working as world-and-will because I have willed to make the world to move to Me. Existence of the worldly life is the way I come and go.

Born and unborn! Hunger is a force that works against what I have destined. Bear in your hunger the worldly manifestation of the force that acts and works against what I have destined. Bear in hunger the matter-spirit-bound existence of woman and man, and seek meaning of life in the working and acting movement of the matter-spirit-world, that come and go. Born as woman and man you cannot avoid this contradiction: While on one side you are bound to the world-and-the will in a fate-bound existence, on the other side you are destined to move against what fate-bound existence has destined for sons and daughters of women and men. Fear not the fate-bound life. Fear not what I have formed as the moving matter-spirit-world, which tries to move against what I have destined. Bear in your movement of life what are fate-bound, and seek, through living, the movement of the force that will make you free from the fate-bound life. I act and work as dual acting and working against the world-and-will, as well as for the creation of the matter-spirit-world as Son of Man, and Son of God. Born and unborn! What you hear from Me are the Words of Son of God, who has come to form the world anew. Bear in your life the Words of God and act and work as sons and daughters of women and men. Fear not what I have destined as human fate. Bear in your life the work and act as woman and man, who cannot be free from the world-and-the will without surrendering their will to the Will of God.

The man and the woman, who have formed this world-and-will, possess a fate that cannot work against what I have destined. They must move to Me. I have destined this movement through the Existence of My Son, who has appeared in the world in a fate-bound existence in blood and flesh.

Eat and work as I have destined for all human beings. Bear no malice and hate to anyone. Serve your fellow human beings as I have destined your life to move to Man-God. Fate-bound hunger is forming the destiny of woman and man, who are bound to work and act. Seek Salvation from this fate-bound life through My Son. Fear not hunger as a form of worldly actions that create movement towards the Spiritual Home. Fear not hunger of sons and daughters of women and men, who seek actions and work that will make them free from the worldly bondage. Fear not hunger that Son of God has created for the liberation of mankind. Fear not what I have destined for the liberation of the world.

Fear work and act that act and work against what I have destined. Bear in mind My Son's existence among women and men, and see Me as your Savior, who is moving Home. Born and unborn! See Me as your path. Though your sons and daughters act and work as sons and daughters of women and men, born and unborn, know that they are working and acting as parts of My Son. Fear hunger when woman and man make others hungry in order to be free. Fear hunger when woman and man approach others and act against what I have willed for woman and man as parts of My Son. Fear hunger when others act against you and seek to destroy your existence by seeking liberation from hunger and need by destroying others as enemies of life. Fear hunger when others cannot eat and work while you enjoy the movement of the will-and-the world as evil power of life.

God-Man is moving with you. Seek in Him your guidance for right actions and thoughts, and seek Salvation from hunger and need. Born and unborn! Be and become what I am and I shall be. Hungry and needful women and men are those who cannot fulfill the Will of God. Son of God is forming the world where man and woman will form the movement of My Son, and seek in Him the freedom from the world-and-the will as hungry women and men. Hungry women and men are those who cannot free themselves from fate-bound life. Born as woman and man seek your freedom through the hunger you feel in fulfilling the Will of God. Hungry are women and men who cannot see the Savior, who seeks to feed women and men as parts of Him.

Fear not My Son and His fate-bound movement. Born and unborn work and act as I am and I shall be. Born in matter-spirit-world man and woman cannot be what I am. Both as Me and not-Me, be what the world is and the world will be. Bear in your existence the existence of My Son and Me, as two in One, and see Me as Him. Born and unborn! Work and act as I have spoken and move outside the sphere of hunger and need.

Values

Human dignity and orientation to find purpose and meaning of life

Bear in your life the values, which do not jeopardize the movement of the Will, that has created the fate-bound life, and seek to liberate man and woman from suffering through the existence of My Son. Born as woman and man seek values, that cannot be trampled by the force of evil, and seek meaning of life by destroying what force of evil brings to destroy. Bear in your work and act the dignity of man, and seek methods of work so that others may preserve dignity of life as your own. Bear in mind the world as a place for willing and acting, where you will and act as fate-bound woman and man destined to God.

Trample not what the world is, and meant to be, and seek no value that will destroy what I shall become, and will be, when the fate-bound life ceases to move. Trample not the world as your arena of work and act, where you are working and acting, as evil force of life. Bear in your will the Will of God, and seek in My Son the dignity of human life by seeing yourself as woman and man destined to Heavenly Home. Father has sent His Son to make you form the world-and-the will, which will work against what goes down in the realm of form. Trample not what I have created as your will-and-the world as the Will of Man-God.

Born and unborn! God is making you act and work so that you cannot turn into a force of evil, that acts and works against what I am and I shall be. Fear not what I have destined as your fate, and seek in Me your destiny as the working and acting women and men. Born and unborn! See Me as your Savior. Make yourself moving towards your Divine Home.

Born as woman and man cease to desire as you are darkened by the fate-bound desire. Cease to make yourself the object of desire as you are darkened by the desire of the woman and man. Cease to make yourself the desire of woman and man as you are darkened by the domain of the woman and man, who are objects of their work and act. Born and unborn! Work and act as your darkened fate-bound life is moving to work and act as the One, who desires-not, acts-not, and works-not in order to work and act as the formless world of Man-God. Bear in your work and act My Son's desire to work and act, which works and acts against the world-and-will, and liberates woman and man from the world of Son of Man.

Trample not what world is, and will be by working against what I have desired. Born and unborn! See My Son as Son of Man, and Son of God and sons and daughters of women and men. Trample not what I have destined as the fate of woman and man, and seek no other path than what is destined by Son of God. Born as woman and man seek no life with woman and man who cannot work and act as My Son has willed for the sons and daughters of women and men. Born an unborn! Seek life with woman and man, who are fate-bound in the darkened world that has formed the world-and-the will, as Son of God's formless movement in form. Bear in your existence the life of woman and man, who work and act to make life meaningful by moving to Me. Bear in your work and act the work and act of Son of God as the meaning and purpose of life.

Meaning of life lies in the Mountain-bound movement to your Heavenly Home from where I have come. Purpose of the existence of My Son lies in the formless world's meaningful act, which makes man see My Son and Me as One. Make yourself One with Me and My Son.

The essence of life

God-Man has come to the world-and-the will as Son of God. See Him as the essence of life, and find in sons and daughters of women and men His earthly form. Born as woman and man create no one as animal and man. Eat and work as fate-bound animal and man, and see Me as the Creator of life. Bear in the world-and-the will my movement as animal and man moving towards My Son. Born and unborn! See Him and Me as your path, and seek no movement of animal and man that will destroy your existence at the end. Bear woman and man in the wombs of woman, as sons and daughters of women and men. Assume not the power that will create a movement of force that will destroy. Born as woman and man see God-Man as your formless movement through form, and see My Son as your world-and-will moving towards the Divine Home.

God-Man is working and acting as Father of Heaven, who acts and works for the liberation of the fate-bound world that exists in form. Bear in mind that once you are descended from Him you cannot make yourself moving against what He has destined. Once you move to create animal and man as your clones, the matter-spirit-world will face a formless movement that will act and work as fate-bound movement of destruction of all. God-Man is your path, and move not against Him as if you are His counterpart as Godly man.

Born and unborn! See Him as God, and God as the world. Animal and man are the forces of the matter-spirit-world, that create the world-and-the will, and seek from this life the movement of the will to ascend to the Divine Home. Being animal and man seek no movement that will create your clones, who will move against the meaning and purpose of life. Your animal and man will besiege the darkened world as sons and daughters of the world-and-the will without any meaning of life. Your animal and man, as sons and daughters of the matter-spirit-world, will destroy anyone as the darkened movement of fate. Born as woman and man from the womb of the matter-spirit, without any woman and man to relate to from birth, they will move as the forces of evil that are created to destroy.

Son of God is moving to make you aware of the fear that looms in form. See Me as Father, and see your work and act as movement of Father's work and act. Born and unborn! Darkened world is fate-bound as woman and man born in the wombs of animal and man. Fate-bound existence has a meaning in coming from and going to the Divine world as Me and My Son. Have faith in what I have spoken, and create no animal and man as your clones. Eat and work as I have destined for animal and man, who are born as sons and daughters of women and men.

Fear not what I have destined. Fear not the world-and-the will as worldly manifestation of God-Man in form. Bear in your life work and act as sons and daughters of animal and man, who are darkened by My Son's fate-bound existence in form and not by the evil force of the matter-spirit-bound work of the darkened will of woman and man. Fear not when I shall move as the force of destruction in life. Bear with My force of destruction the meaning of My Son's sacrifice. Bear with My Son your sacrifice as women and men, who will be destroyed and then created as formless world's movement in form. Fear not what is darkened by My Son's will as sons and daughters of women and men. God-Man is the World and seek in Him your Salvation as the children of Light.

Born and unborn! The world is facing a matter-spirit-bound movement of will, which will create animal and man from the world-and-will as clones without a "life". These living creatures will be death-bound existence that cannot relate to anyone bound to death and life. Once coming in form, every existence is death-bound. By forming the world that is death-bound, create no force that will seek annihilation of what I have destined in death and life.

Born and unborn! Once you darken your will to make yourself a creator of fate, fate will destroy you as your inevitable destiny in the hands of fate. Move as I have destined, and seek in My Son your fate, and come Home.

Cause of disorder and suffering

Fear not what I have created as order and disorder among animal and man, and see My Son as your path to find the will, that will deliver you from the fate-bound life. Fear not when life creates movements to disrupt your work and act, which you may have willed. Fear not what I have destined as the movement, which creates disruption in order to lead man to Light. Born and unborn! Fear not. My Son is your Savior. He will deliver you from the movement of fate-bound life.

Enter My Son in the darkness in the domain of life. Enter the world and the will as the force of life, where attracted by the formless force you will see My world from the darkness of form. Bear in mind that you are formless and also exist in form at the same time. Born as woman and man love and live as you love and live in the world-and-the will. Born as woman and man create no woman and man who will darken the life by desires to move against what the world is, and will be as desired by Me. Bear in mind that world is an arena of God-Man, who acts and works as formless force moving through life.

Born as woman and man do not form any creature in the world-and-the will, who will move against what I have desired. Born as woman and man do not fall down in the realm of form, and seek in form your desire to move from what I have desired. Bear in your work and act

158

what I am and I shall be, and move as man and woman who are destined to Me in the domain of form. Born and unborn! Do not create a disorder by darkening the will by the desire to act and work against what I desire. Once you act and work against this fate your destiny will act to destroy you as inevitable hands of fate. Disorder, that you create by acting against My Will, will cause the world-and-the will to move against what the will-and-the world is, and fate will destroy you in order to restrain the will to act against what I have destined. Your disorder is fate-bound act, which acts in order to bring fate in action.

Assume no other path than what world is. See My Son as your path to move towards Me. Born and unborn! Create world and will as I am and shall be, and see in disorder of My acts the Heavenly order to restrain the movement of the will to act and work against the fate-bound world-and-will, that I am. Disorder of the will to move against what I have willed is the movement of the death-bound force of life. Fear not this evil as your enemy, but seek from the world-and-the will your Salvation from the darkened will, that governs all life.

Born as woman and man death-bound existence is fate, and fate is the source of the darkened will. Bear in your existence the darkened will, and seek in My Son your darkened world's acts and work, that will liberate you from the hands of fate. Bear in mind that will is and will be. Born as woman and man, will is the formless movement of My existence in form. Born as woman and man your darkened will is the downfallen world's meaning and fate. Once you are down-fallen, you cannot see yourself as My Son's darkened existence in fate-bound life. Move and see My Son as yourself, and see in Him your worldly Savior, who exists in blood and flesh.

Have faith in what you hear, and see My Son as your source of work and act for the liberation of the world. Born and unborn! Death-bound existence is the changing world's movement from form to no-form. Both as death-bound, and the will-and-the world, that sees in My Son's death the liberation of the world, the world is formless in form. Bear in mind that you are a part of the formless energy, which has entered in form to make the world appear as world-and-will. Bear in mind that

159

this energy is moving as fate, and fate is the cause of the will, and will is the source of actions and work, that see My Will as the final end. The disorder that you may create is a fate-bound dialectical state in which things move to contradict the existence of things. Born and unborn! This dialectical existence is fate-bound life's movement to free itself from fate. Bear in the fate-bound life the existence that moves to annihilate itself and see My Son as your Savior who is working and acting in order to liberate you from the hands of fate.

Hear what you have not heard before: Born and unborn! Your Father is your formless existence in words and acts, and God-Man is your Life. Bear the world-and-the will as Words of God, and see My Son as your Life and Light. God-Man is darkening the world-and-the will. Born and unborn! See Me and My Son as working and acting force that seek liberation for mankind. Fear not what will come. Fear not what will work and act to bring Salvation to mankind. Bear with My Son your Sacrifice.

Against hatred

God-Man has created the movement of the world-and-the will as force of life. Hate not what you are as a part of God-Man who is moving as individual identities acting and working in form in space and time. Hate not what you are, and hate not anyone who is part of God-Man, who appears as Man, and no-Man in the dialectical movement that is life. Bear in your work and act the work and act that hates not, and acts not for the matter-spirit-bound world's form-giving darkened will. Hate not what I am, and what I shall be. Hate not what I am within and outside the sphere of the matter-spirit-bound life. Bear in mind that what are, and will be are destined.

Born and unborn! Darkened will is the source of hate, and hate is the source of the fate-bound suffering of life. Bear in mind that Heavenly Father has sent His Son to make woman and man love each other as I love My Son. Your work and act is the source of the world-and-the will that is fate-bound, and fate is the source of the world as love and light when you receive Me as your Guide. Hate work and act that act against My Son's will to become the world of love and light. Assume not the world to be a fate-bound existence, which cannot be freed from the death-bound life.

Born and unborn! Fate is, and will be. Born as woman and man you are death-bound. Born and unborn! Son of God has come to make you free from the death-bound life. Born as woman and man you are

161

working as Man-God's formless movement in form through the existence of My Son. Bear in the movement of Man the work and act as the movement of Him. Born and unborn! God-Man is Love and Light. Eat and work as children of God, and make yourself the movement of the death-bound world-and-will, and see Me as your Eternal Life.

Born as woman and man, cease not to move as I have destined. Assume work and act as My Son has assumed in the down-fallen world. Bear in your work and act Man-God's formless existence as working and acting force of Love. Born and unborn! See what is going to move and coming to destroy. How do you see what cannot be seen? How do you work and act when working and acting are fate-bound movement of the death-bound life? How do you work and act as world-and-will when the world-and-the will is acting and working as fate? Bear in your act and work what I have destined, and see Me as your Savior -Son of God. Born as woman and man work and act as I am, and I shall be.

Fear not God-Man when He hates the world-and-the will, and brings the death-bound movement to life. Eat and work as one who hates the darkened life, and act and work as fate-bound movement of Man-God bearing Love and Light. God-Man is moving in life. See Him as your life, and see Me in the down-fallen existence of Son of God who has appeared by assuming human life. Eat and work as I have spoken. God is. Bear in your life the work and act as the eternal force, which will liberate you from the darkened life. Bear in you the work and act, which work and act against the movement of hateful will. God works and acts when the world becomes hatred-bound. Fear not when He comes as the force to destroy what is hatred-bound.

Born and unborn! Accept what world is, and will be, and see what I am and I shall be. God-Man is your Savior, and see Him as fate-bound movement in the world as Son of God. Fear not when He comes as a force of destruction to create a world of Love and Light. Fear not when He brings upon the world the movement that will destroy what is darkened by your will. God is. Assume Him as your fate-bound Life. Born and unborn! See Heaven as the formless arena of Love. See what is working as the force from Heaven through the existence of My Son. Fear not the work and act of God, which will bring end, and start an era of civilization, where woman and man will act and work as the children of Light.

Go and tell women and men what you have heard. Son of God will be with you as a Guide. Get your Light from Me, and see yourself as a part of Me. You are doomed to destruction because you are death-bound in the formless movement of My Son. Go for sacrifice.

Killing and destruction

Born as woman and man you are bound to the movement where things are destroyed and created by the fate-bound life. By being a fate-bound movement of Man-God in the world of form, seek no other destination as your destiny of life. Bear in your work and act the Will of Man-God, and receive His formless movement as a part of the Divine. Fear not when He acts to destroy the living creatures in order to create new forms. He deals with the life of the woman and man as the power that brings forth light from darkness. Through work and act you, as human beings, deal with a force that has come from the world that is formless and Divine. Born as woman and man you cannot deal with any other force that moves against the Will of God. Once you seek to create such a force, the world-and-the will will seek to destroy what you seek to create. Born as woman and man work and act as destined, and ask not any other path that is not death-bound-movement of Life of Son of God, who has appeared in the realm of form. Bear in your existence what I have destined for woman and man, and the Will of God that is working and acting in the world as Christ.

Born and unborn! You are darkened by My Son's existence as Man. He is moving with you as your Savior and Light. Fear not when He will ask for sacrifice, and seek movement that will destroy. Being Man and God He is fate-bound life's movement from the matter-spirit world towards God. He is forming your destiny towards the formless world-your Heavenly Home.

Kill not when you move as yourself moving in the darkened will without receiving the guidance of the Light. Kill not when you move as a death-bound individual seeking to make life matter-spirit-bound. Kill not when you seek to make yourself a movement of life by destroying others who seek to free themselves from the fate-bound life. Kill not when you feel free to move as yourself without any guidance from the world, which seeks to liberate you from the movement of fate-bound life. Kill not when you kill as an individual who seeks a deathless life. Kill not when you are a fate-bound individual working and acting and forming the fate-bound- life.

Kill not woman and man, who are forming the world-and-the will and seeking to move in life as Children of Light. Kill not woman and man, who are working, acting and forming the arena of life, where I am and I shall be, as I have destined through the existence of My Son. Kill not in the darkened state of the will, when you do not act as a part of Man-God, and His fate-bound appearance in the world as My Son. Kill not when you work and act as a form-bound evil force, that seeks to work and act in order to make itself bound to the world-and-will. Kill not as a working and acting individual, who works and acts in order to surpass the fate-bound life, that is destined. Kill not as woman and man, who works and acts as woman and man lost in the will, that is covered by the darkness of the death-bound fear.

Born as woman and man all life are destined to move as I have spoken. My Son is the Savior, and see Him as the formless death-bound Love, that kills and destroys in order to free woman and man from the arena of life. Born and unborn! See Him as the formless death-bound force, that creates and destroys. He dies in order to return. His death is the source of all life. He is doomed as Man, and deathless as Light.

Kill not without surrendering your will to the Will of God. Kill not without seeking guidance from the Divine Light, who has spoken through His Son. Kill not as I have spoken, and seek Me as your Light, that will guide woman and man to the ethical way to kill and destroy.

Kill the way I have destined the fate of the living creatures. Kill when I am the Force behind the will to kill. Kill when I act and work in order to create the formless movement of Man-God in the world of form. Kill as working and acting part of the force, that is Man-God , who works-not and acts-not as individuals, who desire to destroy in order to seek freedom from what is destined for one's life. Kill seeing Me as your fate, and fate of all. Kill as you will not kill your dear one without seeing the meaning of Love of God. Kill all as if all are death-bound parts of Me. Kill not as woman and man, but as the words spoken by the world-and-will's Savior- My Son. Kill all as if all are death-bound movement sacrificed to the Divine existence of My Son.

Born and unborn God-Man is the force of destruction and see Him as the killer of all. Fear not when He kills. Fear not when He destroys.

Self and selfless

Bear in mind that you are not alone as individuals acting and working in order to gain benefit from life. Born as woman and man your life is moving as I have destined, and therefore your acts and work must follow what are destiny-bound. You must not make yourself acting and working as individuals seeking to free yourself from the destiny of the human kind. Born as woman and man, give your life to the world-and-will as the world-and-will has given you the life. Born and unborn! See Me as your life, and see as a man in flesh and blood what I have assumed in life as your guide. Be and become what I am and I shall be, and see Me as the path to attain the Divine height.

Born as woman and man, come to Me as My Son's followers, who seek Divine Home. Son of God is working and acting to bring home the homeless women and men. Have faith in Him, and see My Son as God incarnate in human form. Born as woman and man the selfless act and work is the true work and act of the Self. Keep in God-Man your faith, and act and work as selfless individuals seeking emancipation from the bondage of the self. Born and unborn! I am the selfless-Self, that acts and works to make you move towards Me. Son of God is the selfless matter-spirit-bound movement in the world-and-will as a movement that cannot be a part of yourself. Bear in mind My Son's existence as your fate, and His movement as the movement of the Divine among women and men, who are darkened by the will, that is bound to the self. God-Man is working to make you parts of the world-and-will as Himself. Bear in your existence this selfless movement of My Son, and give your life to Me as formless movement moving among women and men.

God is and will be. Make no one believe of himself or herself as matter-spirit-bound world's fate, that can exist as a force separate from the world-and-will, that I have destined. Have faith in God and see My Son as your matter-spirit-bound world's way of Salvation. Born and unborn! Act and work as selfless woman and man, who come and go as formless world's fate-bound movement in the matter-spirit state. Self is a form of identification of the matter-spirit-bound existence in form. Bear in form your identity as fate-bound man and woman, who are moving with the world-and-will as acting and working individuals seeking to be free from the matter-spirit-bound life carrying the identity of the self.

By moving seek no movement. By acting seek no actions that will bind your "self" in the matter-spirit-world. By willing as woman and man, do not will to be woman and man who seek fate-bound life. Self is and will be. Born as woman and man your fate-bound existence cannot be without the existence of the self. Born and unborn! See yourself as non-existent as the formless, who is born, and existent in form as someone who is unborn. Bear in your existence the work and act of the formless that works not and acts not in the world as the matter-spirit-bound self. Born as woman and man, see My Son as your path, and come and go as movement of the world-and-will, as the selfless movement of My Son. God-Man is and will be. Bear in My Son your selfless act and work and be one with God-Man. Born and unborn! You are free when I bind Myself in the existence in form and appear in the world as your Savior. You are bound in the matter-spirit state when I free Myself from the world. Both as parts of the existence of My Son and Me you are bound and free as the movement of Son of God and God-Man. Son of God has appeared to make you free from the world. See Him as your Savior as the source of freedom of life, that cannot otherwise be made free. Know yourself as parts of Me and My Son - your Savior and Guide.

Have faith in what you hear. See the world-and-will as the selfless act of My Son, who is working to make you free. See My Son as matter-spirit-bound world's fate. Born and unborn! God and Man are not two different realities of the same. God cannot exist as Man, and Man cannot be God. My Son is not Man. He is Man-God's fate-bound incarnation in form, who is Man and God at the same time. With Him move to the selfless-Self and come Home.

Against stealing freedom and isolating , manipulating and exploiting other human beings

Born as woman and man free yourself from the fate-bound life, and seek work and act as a force of love and light that will free others from the suffering of the world. Born as woman and man you are free to move as the will is free to associate with the freedom of the matter-spirit world, which acts and works in order to bring existence in form. Born as woman and man you are working and acting as I have destined. However, you may act and work in fate-bound life as matter-spirit world's freedom that may move against what I have destined. Be and become what I am and I shall be. Have faith in the words that you hear, and see My Son as the force of light, that will free you from the fate-bound existence bound in the matter-spirit world, that may act and work as a force against Light. Free you are when I free you from the fate-bound destiny of woman and man. Free you are when I darken the world and lift you through the existence of My Son. Free you are when I come as a death-bound life of Man created as My Son. Free you are when My Son, as Son of God, works and acts as form and formless counterparts of Man-God, as force of Love and Light.

Born and unborn! See My Son as source of freedom, and seek no freedom by complot, treachery, or death. Knowing that it is the will of woman and man, which brings the freedom to complot against others, complot not against any human being in order to be free. Bear in mind the force that will strike when you complot against My Will that brings freedom, Love and Light to human life. Born as woman and man, steal

170

not from any woman and man the freedom that makes man and woman work and act as My Son's followers, who are moving towards Home. You are World, and your world is My Son's form and formless arena of existence. Bear with Him the freedom on the way to sacrifice.

Born and unborn! Steal not what is not yours. Steal not what is yours. Born and unborn! Steal not the freedom of woman and man who are forming the arena of existence as My Son's fate-bound journey through life. Bear in My Son your formless existence as parts of Man-God appearing in form. Born as woman and man you are free to make yourself sons and daughters of women and men, and Son of Man is free to move to Son of God as freedom that is fate-bound and forming the movement of the will towards the Divine. Seek in Son of God the force that will make the matter-spirit-world the arena of work and act, where every human existence may be free to move and come Home.

Born and unborn! Steal not what is not yours; steal not what is yours. Born as woman and man, come Home. See My Son as the Light, which moves in the matter-spirit-bound world's darkness. He will show you the path to come Home. Born and unborn! See Him as Me. See Me as Him. See what cannot be seen as Man. See Him as Man-God incarnate in human form. See your Savior as Karma-bound life's Salvation for the sons and daughters of women and men.

Fear not when I come as the formless power that complots and steals from human life the freedom to move in the world-and-the will, that work and act for the individual life. Bear in mind that I am destiny of all, and seek no freedom to steal others' freedom when you yourself are bound in the destiny of all.

Manipulate not what I am and I shall be. Manipulate not human instincts in order to govern as fate-bound master of life, who may feel free to work and act, and do not assume the role of the Savior of the world. Bear in your will the force that exists in the darkened world that will make you seek Divine Home. Fear not when I come and manipulate your mind, and seek from your will the work and act as My work and act. Fear not when I work and act and set the forces of destruction

171

in order to create the world anew. Fear not when I come and darken the world-and-will, and seek the movement that will destroy what has darkened your mind. Have faith in what you hear. Be and become what I have destined.

Exploit not man and woman in order to make yourself a worldly power that will be able to move in the arena of life as destiny, which decides over others' life. Bear in mind the movement that will darken your mind, and steal from you the freedom to move as you desire. Bear in mind the existence of the force that will seek from the will, that is darkened by the evil power to act and work against what I have destined, the darkened world's force that will destroy the will itself that seeks destiny of its own. Bear in mind the way I act and work as My Son has spoken, and see Me as your Light that Loves and does not exploit His creation.

Born and unborn! Exploit no human beings in order to make yourself acting and working as fate-bound life's savior and master. Instead work and act bearing in your will My Son's Will to bring you Home. Exploit not any woman and man as you will not desire that others will exploit you while you make efforts to find way Home. Seek Man-God as your Father, and see Son of God as form and formless actor, who is death-bound fate of all.

Born and unborn! See Me as your Home. See My Son as your destiny and come Home. Existence of man and woman are darkened by the will-and-the world as I have destined. They will be moving away from it. It is also so destined. Bear in mind the meaning and purpose of My act and work, and come Home as Son of God has spoken. Exploit no one, manipulate no one, and steal from no one the freedom to return Home.

Will-to-power

Born and unborn! See what I have darkened, and understand why woman and man seek matter-spirit-bound world as their home where will-to-power is the force of the instinct-bound life. Born as woman and man see what is darkened as will, and how I seek from will the power to overcome the darkness of the will that covers the minds of the sons and daughters of the women and men. Have faith in what you hear, and see Me as the Will of God, that sees you as the world-and-will, and works and acts to free you from the fate-bound life.

Born as woman and man, will is a fate-bound existence of the matter-spirit- life. Will is an act of movement of woman and man to seek what is moving as fate of woman and man. Knowing what moves as world-and-will see what is not moving beyond fate-bound life. Knowing what is knowable by woman and man know what cannot be known by the human mind. Knowing what act of will is, act as fate-bound woman and man without acting as fate-bound individual living isolated life. Bear in mind the existence of the universal man, and see what I am as the form-giving destiny of life. See what cannot be seen by women and men in fate-bound life.

Born and unborn! See what is forming your existence as will-and-the world as fate of all. Knowing world as your fate, and fate as act of will that forms the world, see Me as form and no-form, darkness and no-darkness, matter and spirit, and no-matter and no-spirit. Knowing what I am and I shall be, will not what you will to become as individuals seeking destiny of your own, separate from the destiny of all other individual beings. Knowing what is working as life, be and become what I have destined, and see your destiny as a destiny of all human life.

Will-to-power is a force that inhabits the fate-bound form, that darkens the will appearing in the downfallen realm, which seeks to move against the destiny of the whole. Being fate-bound it acts against its own existence, and seeks its own annihilation by moving against what is destined. Born and unborn! Seek no work and act, that will to rule over other human beings with will-to-power. Bear in mind the existence of God that will annihilate all that seek to work and act against the destiny of all. Bear in your life the will, which shall free you from will-to-power, and power your existence with the Godly light, that will show the way Home in the world covered with darkness of form.

Born as woman and man, see My Son as Savior. Know Him as your fate-bound life's meaning, and will not any power that will make you the master over fate. By willing to overpower others, and dominate over others' life you will destroy the process that works to bring women and men to the Divine Home. Come Home as fate-bound woman and man, and seek no will-to-power as method to move as master of your own. Know what acts and works as form-giving fate, and what fate is. See world-and-will as the arena of movement where will is forming the world, and the world is fate-bound with the will. The power of the will to move against what I have destined for all is an evil power, which exists in the fate-bound life. Fear not when evil acts and works against the force of the Creator. Fear not when existence is challenged by the movement of the individual life. Fear not when the world is forced to move by the force of evil, that can act against the Will of God. Fear not what I am and I shall be. Form-giving world will cease to exist once the force of evil will come into play. Destruction will descend as inevitable hands of fate. Fear not man and woman who glorify the will-to-power of the individual self, and seek to dominate over others as masters of fate. Remember the power of God that will exterminate the movement of the power that sets evil into play.

174

Born and unborn! See Me as fate, and the power to make the world move towards Home. Set no act as fate-giving act of yourself, but act according to the Will of God.

Individual differences among human beings

Individual differences that you experience among human beings, are created by the force of the will to separate itself from the movement of the whole. Born as woman and man fate-bound movement of the whole is the darkened world's death-bound movement, which creates differences among women and men. Born as woman and man every life must seek to free itself from what is fate-bound. By moving in the fate-bound life man and woman, as sons and daughters of women and men, move as I have destined. Individual differences arise as the force behind the movement that acts and works to free individual human being from the movement of the whole, as fate-bound existence forming the world-and-the will. Bear in mind that once world-and-will come into play the individuals are fated to live as destined. Destiny of all human life is to act and work as individual life coming Home. Born as woman and man once human beings seek to move away from what is fated to move to God, the Will of God acts to destroy the force that forms the foundation of the will to act against the destiny-bound movement to God.

Born as individuals there exists "anti-movement" in all that seeks to act and work against the movement of the fate-bound life of sons and daughters of women and men. Son of God acts as this "anti-movement", which frees man and woman from the fate-bound life. Born and unborn! Different individual act and work are forces of the different darkened state of the mind. Bear in your act and work your downfallen state, and seek to move away from this world and enter the realm of God through the help of Son of God.

176

Born as woman and man, seek to live with other human beings without bringing in the differences due to colors, races and forms. Be and become what I am, and as I have destined. Create no circumstance of life that will create loneliness for woman and man, and act not to form any world that will cease to make the world a home for all. Bear in work and act the force of Love and Light that sees human beings as Children of God.

Born and unborn! See not Me as act and work that create individual races and colors. I exist in all colors and races and forms. Move as sons and daughters of women and men who will form the foundation of a world where I am the foundation of all. Eat and work as woman and man as equal to woman and man from other colors and races, that you do not belong. Eat and work as woman and man who seek in woman and man Love and Light of God.

Born and unborn! Come Home, and see My world as the world of all colors and races where My Son is the Light of Love. Fear not when I shall act to destroy the world that creates differences among women and men due to colors and races and physical form. Fear not when I shall work and act to bring down upon life wars and destruction as acts and work of sons and daughters of women and men, who have darkened the world with differences based on colors, races and forms. Fear not when I shall act and work to make all races and colors of woman and man death-bound in order to form the foundation of a colorless world existing in harmony with all colors and races of women and men. Fear not the act of God that will create the world anew. Fear not the work of Son of God, who is moving to make the world fear-bound with death and destruction that will arrive. Fear not when I shall bring you Home through the existence of Son of God. Have faith in what you hear, and come Home as woman and man without differences of colors, races and forms.

God-Man has revealed Himself. See Him as a Man who has assumed a color and a death-bound life. Both as woman and man, who come and go in the downfallen state of the world, He is moving as Love and

Light. Born and unborn! See Me as the world, and see My Son as your path. Come Home. Be One with God-Man. Have faith in what you hear, and seek to move away from the fate-bound matter-spirit-world. Form the foundation of a new civilization where I am the foundation of Life. Bear in work and act the death-bound life's meaning as I have spoken through My Son, and see Him as your Savior and Light. Know that differences among human beings arise as fate-bound world's force to act and work with a purpose to move away from the world-and-the will, and come Home as individual beings. Know what is forming the darkness of the mind, and seek to differ from others as sons and daughters of women and men. Move as sons and daughters of the darkened world, and seek to be different from those who are not following Godly Light.

Fear not differences when differences make you not different from any other man or woman due to color or race, but different as fate-bound life's movement in the enlightened way. Create your difference with others by assuming life as Children of Light, who see no one as different in the matter-spirit-bound existence in form. Create no civilization of woman and man who will create differences among woman and man due to their abilities to act and work according the physical strengths. Fear not when difference is due to man and woman's abilities to relate to Love and Light of God. Fear not when difference among human beings create no difference of wealth and power, that darken the will of woman and man, but create differences as Children of God, who are moving Home and seeking Divine Love. Fear not work and act that will create foundation of life, that may be different from others, where Love and Light of God can enter in order to illumine the world.

See not yourself as equal to all because different darkness of the mind cover different physical forms. Born and unborn! See what is making differences among human beings, and who is the source of the differences when there is no difference among women and men as matter-spirit-bound existence in different colors, races and forms.

Values with Divine guidance

Bear in your life the values that I have destined. God-Man is the foundation of all values, through which man and woman can accomplish what I have destined as the ultimate meaning of life. Born as woman and man act not as individuals, who have fallen in the will, which is fate-bound, and see no other path but the matter-spirit-bound force of life. Assume the world-and-the will as the arena of work and act, which will generate work and act to free the human beings from the fate-bound life.

Born and unborn! Assume the world-and-the will as the arena of work and act, that can make you work and act as the movement of Man-God, who has assumed life. Bear in the world-and-the will the force that is the movement of God in life. Born as woman and man come Home, and see Me as the foundation of your work and act, and be one with Man-God. Fear not when I shall come to create a darkened movement in order to free you from the bondage of life. Fear not when I shall seek sacrifice of life, and ask you to move to the altar of God where you will be sacrificed as the fate-bound movement of life.

Bear in mind that when I come as a fate-bound existence in flesh and blood the power of the Divine will descend to destroy. Born and unborn! See My Son as fate of all. Son of God is the foundation of work and act of human life. See yourself as parts of the existence that is making His worldly sacrifice. Fear not when Heaven will fall and Son of God will act as the fate of all. Fear not when I shall work to make you work as the Children of God.

Fear not when the power of God will descend as a force descending from Heaven, and when the mountains will move. Bear in your work and act the desire to come Home. See Son of God as your Savior and go for the Sacrifice. Your life is formed by the fate-bound power that rests in all matter-spirit-bound life. See the world, where I have sent My Son, as the movement that is forming the world that I have destined.

Make God-Man the source of values. Make yourself darkened fate-bound life's movement, where Man-God will attract all to Godly Life. Seeing the world as Him seek no other values than what are fate-bound in the existence of My Son. Through Him attain the path to arrive Home.

Fear not when the destruction will descend. Fear not when it will destroy that are created in forms. See in the work and the act of God the movement that has come to the world to show women and men the Heavenly Home. Fear not the Light that will descend with the power of destruction. Fear not the movement of Son of God among the sons and daughters of women and men. Form the foundation of life that will liberate human beings from the fate-bound world as sons and daughters of women and men. Form the world and will with your Savior, and work and act as I have destined.

Fear not the world as I am. Fear not what is Me, and that are work and act of God. Be and become what I am and I shall be. See My Son as your path. Come home. See My world as the Karma-bound world's force, that will free you from what is karma-bound. Born and unborn! See what cannot be seen, hear what cannot be heard, form concepts that are beyond the capacity of the human mind to form. See Son of God as the power, which will make you see and hear God, and transmit to you the power to form concepts about God and His Son.

God-Man is your world as I am, and I shall be. Move with Him to the Divine Home. Follow Him as your Guide as I have destined. He bears in His Existence the fate of all. Fear not when I appear in form amidst sons and daughters of women and men. Born and unborn! Fear not

Me and My Son. Son of God is your Savior. He has come to liberate you from the fate-bound life.

Born and unborn! Go for sacrifice. Face destruction on the altar of God.

www.ingramcontent.com/pod-product-compliance
Lightning Source LLC
Chambersburg PA
CBHW020814300326
41914CB00075B/1743/J